Praise for Lisa Schiller

"In 'Borrowing Hope', Lisa brings us into her life in such detail that you, the reader, will be exposed to almost every fear you may harbor: major illness, job loss, financial and emotional insecurity; going from the top in your profession to fighting to survive at the bottom. With each chapter, you will see how Lisa overcomes the obstacle, beats the odds, while openly sharing the wisdom she accrues along the way. But before you begin the first chapter of 'Borrowing Hope,' may I recommend you track down Rachel Platten's 'Fight Song' and listen carefully to the lyrics. This song may be Lisa's anthem, but I have a feeling she won't mind sharing."

Terry L. Murphy,
Editor, Cambridge, Massachusetts
Former Editor, Gannett Newspapers, Boston Herald

"Lisa Schiller's book, 'Borrowing Hope,' is a testament to the human spirit. Her story reminds us to keep going, no matter the odds. She has experienced great highs and lows in her life but has never lost sight of the importance of family, friends, and her God. Lisa has lived life to the fullest, walking through pain, fear, and several near-death experiences. Each time she has taken something from those experiences to continue her path with an open heart and her willingness to give back to others. It is a book that will help you put your life in perspective, will offer one hope, and open your world to possibilities you might not have seen before... It'll make a great movie!"

Bill Robertson
Writer/Producer, Los Angeles, CA

Borrowing Hope

Lisa Schiller

Cover design by Holly Bloom-Ranieri
Editor: Susan Smith Editor: Terry Murphy
Photographer: Kajal Schiller
Printed by TimberKnoll's Spirit Cove, Inc
563 Orangewood Lane, Dandridge, TN 37725 United States
Newfietherapy.org   First Printing edition 2020
It is important to note that events in the book are from the author's memories from her perspective. The author has tried to recreate events, locales, and conversations from her memories that may be inexact due to her recuperation from major brain surgery. In order to maintain their anonymity in some instances, she has changed the names of individuals and some identifying characteristics to protect the identities of those involved. Although the author and publisher have made every effort to ensure that the information in this book was correct at press time, the author and publisher do not assume and hereby disclaim any liability to any party for any loss, damage, or disruption caused by errors or omissions, whether such errors or omissions result from negligence, accident, or any other cause.

TimberKnoll's Spirit Cove is committed to publishing works that are uplifting and spread kindness, hope, and love. In that spirit, we have published this book for you, the audience; however, the story, the experiences, and the words are the author's alone.

For my daughter, Kajal

You are the center of my world. You grew in my heart long before we met, and being your mother is the greatest gift I could ever have imagined. You had faith I would survive when nobody else did; you are wise beyond your years, and the world is a more breathtaking place because you are in it. You inspire me every day, with your strength, your clarity, and your humor. I will always love you, forever and ever.

Acknowledgments

I would not have survived the past few years without learning to accept help from those who showed up for me when my life was on the line.

If not for my brother, Phil, and his good friend Eddie making the arrangements for the world-class surgical team at The Duke Medical Center, I would not be here today. To my little brother, Brad, who put his Doctor hat on by quietly taking over my medical care and not hesitating to be there when I needed you, thank you.

To Dr. Henry Friedman and Dr. Allen Friedman, your brilliance knows no bounds. I will forever be grateful for your world-class surgical skills and cutting-edge brain tumor research. You are saving lives and creating hope where little hope may otherwise exist. Thank you for a second chance at life. Dr. Jovan Markovich, you were there by my side from before my craniotomy to when I left the hospital. Your patience in answering my questions repeatedly, when I could not remember what you had told me five minutes earlier, was incredible. Susan Barrella, your nursing skills, understanding of brain surgery, and endless compassion helped guide me through recovery, thank you. To all the surgeons and nurses who work so diligently to save lives at The Preston Robert Tisch Brain Tumor Center, thank you.

To my mother, who raised me to believe that I could overcome any obstacle, my sister Linda, for being there when everything went to hell and for being such an inspiration, I love you so much. To Lizzie, you will always be my 'baby' sister, thank you for being there with a prayer and a kind word, no matter what life throws at me. To my father, who took the time in his final days to tell me he was proud of me and reaffirmed that my daughter was all Schiller, no matter where she was born, you'll always be in our hearts.

To Patti and Benita and our magnificent Newfoundland family, thank you for trusting us with your cherished Newfie puppies. They have lighted up our lives and our hearts in more ways than we ever could have imagined. You are the best Newfie breeders anyone could hope to find, and without you, TimberKnoll's Spirit Cove would not exist. You have helped me find a new purpose, and together, we will bring stress relief and healing through pet therapy to so many who desperately need it.

To the Hudson Ambassadors, thank you for your commitment to helping others and all the hours you spend learning water rescue and therapy training. You and our Newfies are the heart of Spirit Cove.

To Dr. William Burke, you gave me more than this title. You gave me hope when all I could see was a future of pain and darkness.

To my editors, Susan Smith, and Terry Murphy, thank you for helping me put my story to paper. You never stopped believing that I should write this book, and without you, I would not have. Thank you for having faith in me.

Joanne and Nicholas, Woody, and Plato thank you for introducing us to Newfies in the first place. Our love of these magnificent bear size dogs, with flying fur and drool, has brought us more joy than we ever could have imagined!

Bill and Liz, thank you for reminding me that miracles happen even when the miraculous seems beyond our reach. That all we need to do is remember one special prayer and to take life, one day at a time.

To Pastor Ryan and Seacoast Church, thank you for convincing me that God was not done with me yet.

To Kelly, Raider, and all therapy dogs and handlers in the world that donate their time to make the world a brighter place for so many, thank you.

To Patty and Matt, you helped my family at a time when I didn't know how to help myself, and you got us up the mountain, which put Chewie in my arms and opened us up to the world of pet therapy, thank you.

To John Stagliano, thank you for the best brownies and 'sauce' in the world and for introducing me to raspberry lemonade and Rachel Platten, whose 'Fight Song' got me through more frightening times than you could ever imagine.

To Steven Sharp Nelson and the Piano Guys, thank you for all the faith and beauty you put into your music. It was all I could listen too or watch in the darkest and most painful days of my illness. Your music soothed my mind and, more importantly, my soul. Your dedication in Charleston, of 'The Fight Song,' is a memory my daughter and I will cherish forever.

To Holly Bloom-Raineri, my soul sister… you have been my best friend since first grade, and no matter how many miles separated us, your love was always close. Every person should know what it is like to be so loved and accepted unconditionally.

To all the friends and family who prayed for me, who cooked our dinners and made us laugh, thank you for being so generous and supportive, it truly takes a village, and we are so grateful for ours.

Borrowing Hope

Help!

I s this it? Is this truly the last day of my life? After all the battles I have overcome in life, is this what it comes down to – sitting alone in a darkening medical office having heard the worst diagnosis anyone could ever imagine hearing? I had already survived a fire, category five hurricane, and a mobster boyfriend; this could not be 'it'! Then again, I am guessing that is what everyone thinks when they get bad news, this can't be happening to me. My hands were shaking, and I could not breathe. I was numb all over; was I in shock, or was it more? I was trying to think clearly, but I couldn't. All I could think about at this moment was my daughter. My beautiful, talented, stubborn, convinced she knows more than me about absolutely everything, teenage daughter. How could she lose me when she had already lost one mother, after everything she had survived? God, please don't take me from her now, but as I pleaded, I realized, why would he save me? Was I even worth saving? In my heart, I knew the answer; I was not.

My life truly began with a prayer about 13 years ago. Another relationship with a man I had been sure was 'the one' had just come to an abrupt and disappointing end. I was questioning everything in my life, but mostly, how I'd turned 40 and was still alone and childless. I had always assumed there would be time, and that true love, marriage, and children were just around the corner, but the reality had hit home. My dreams had not, and likely never would come true. In desperation, I pleaded with God. If motherhood was not what you wanted for me, why did you place this desperate aching in my heart? The idea of not having a child when I had always known I wanted to be a mother, was beyond comprehensible. Please, God, just let me know if this is not your plan for me; I will let my dreams of a family go, just tell me, send me a sign. Please!

That night I dreamed of her, of a little girl with shining black hair and brown skin, 4 or 5 years old. She gazed up at me. "Are you my mother?" she asked. "Yes," I answered, and as she ran into my arms, I felt as if I had given birth and knew I loved this child with my whole being. The next morning, I awoke, knowing that God had answered my prayers. I knew without a doubt that my new path was one of adoption, and that somewhere in the world, my daughter awaited. It took me a lot more prayers, hard work, and fearless determination, and almost six years later, I found her in an orphanage in India. Like the dream had portrayed, we were meant to be a family. She was my miracle, and I was hers. When I later reflected on the timing of my dream, I realized it was the month that she was born.

After all, she had survived, the streets of India, starvation, the brutality of her orphanage and abandonment by her birth mother, how could she lose me too? I couldn't think of anything else. I couldn't process what the doctors had told me.

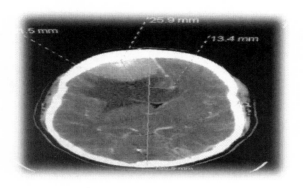

Hidden Enemy

I t must have been growing inside of my head for more than ten years. It was massive. A meningioma, a brain tumor. What? A brain tumor? It was inconceivable, but if I could have thought clearly, I would have realized the signs and symptoms had been there for a long time.

I had developed horrific morning migraines daily, going back over a year, and I had been violently ill from them. I had grown depressed, short-tempered. Even my vision had gotten dramatically worse. I had seen my doctor several times, but she had told me it was all likely due to menopause, and she had never suggested running tests. That morning, as I tried to make my morning coffee, I felt winded. I could not catch my breath, and after popping a few migraine pills when the headaches hit during the day, I decided to stop in urgent care. I had waited until my work for the day was done, and I was able to clear time in the afternoon. A nurse practitioner had seen me, listened to my symptoms, and ordered a CT scan for that evening. As I tried to check out after the procedure, I was told not to leave, that the nurse would be reviewing the results with me by phone. I thought that was strange, but the receptionist assured me it was to give me the results before the upcoming holiday weekend. I grew more stressed as the sky outside the medical facility was growing dark, and all I could think of was that I needed to get home to Kajal, but the receptionist was insistent; it would only be a few more minutes. It didn't feel right, fear started to creep in, and the walls of the waiting room began to close in on me.

When my phone finally rang, and the nurse told me of my diagnosis, it was as if she were talking from a long distance and to someone else. I was alone, holding the phone, sitting in the now darkened medical lobby. I asked her to repeat what she had told me. She suggested texting me the image, so I could look at it, perhaps hoping it would help me understand and process the news, but how could I? I heard the words, but they sounded foreign ... brain tumor. Right frontal lobe? What did that even mean? "Massive," she said... "it's beginning to press on the left side of your brain; it's pushing your brain into your brain stem. It is critical, life-threatening. You need to go to the emergency room; a brain surgeon is waiting for you. Lisa, you need emergency brain surgery." Her words were spinning. "They'll do a craniotomy where they cut open your skull." What? What?! Help! I was screaming in my head, help! It hurts, the pressure in my head got worse. Help! I kept screaming silently; what do I do? What do I do?

I called my brother Brad; he is a doctor. I thought he would know what to do. I can't call my mother, who was at home taking care of my daughter. Oh, my God, Kajal, I cannot be sick, I can't leave her! I knew I would break down if I called them. I could not break down. I had to hold it together and figure out what to do. So, I called Brad, and I repeated what the nurse told me. "No, Lisa, you have it wrong," he reassured me. "This doesn't happen. If this were a meningioma, they would try other things first, not brain surgery. It can't be that bad". I hung on to his words, but I had written down what the nurse told me. I had a sick feeling I hadn't misheard her, but I clung to his disbelief. He promised to call my mother and Kajal, and as I walked out to my car, my feet had trouble moving. I could not see color; the world was suddenly dark and gray.

I managed to open the car door. It seemed heavier than it had earlier today. Was it, or was my mind playing tricks on me? I completely broke down sobbing and had trouble catching my breath. Alone in the car, I just kept replaying the nurse's words in my head, and as I sobbed, I realized these could be the last moments of my life... here in the dark, empty parking lot, grasping for a sense of reality as I sobbed silently. There was a knock

4

on the window, and a woman from the doctor's office was standing there. I struggled to find the right button to roll down the window. It was such a simple thing to do, but my hands were not working. I could not think straight. "Are you alright?" she asked. Can you imagine? Are you all alright? If that was not a ridiculous question. Oh sure, I should have answered, your office just told me I have a killer brain tumor, but hey, what else is new? I'm great; life is just hunky-dory. I am not sure what I said, probably, sure, I'm fine. Isn't that what we always do? Be polite, no matter the situation. It was ridiculous. She handed me the DVD of my brain scan and asked that I bring it with me to the ER.

I knew I should not be driving, I must have been in shock, but I could not find the words to ask for help. Instead, I proceeded to drive myself to the emergency room. It was truly insane. I stopped in the middle of the highway, looking at the entrance to the hospital, not even sure how to turn the wheel. Confused and in a daze, I stared at the red emergency room sign. It called to me, but I was frozen. Traffic passed me by, horns blew, but there I was. Stuck in the middle of the highway in total shock and completely lost as to what to do next.

The Diagnosis

Parking was terrible; I could not help but laugh. Here I was trying to deal with a nightmare prognosis, likely dying and waiting, for what? My brain to stop working? Would I suddenly be unable to breathe, to walk, to function at all? I was not sure what could happen, do brains blow up? Meltdown? This parking situation would undoubtedly give me a stroke. There were no spaces, and I drove in circles. You would think they'd have a valet for a critically ill, emergency patient, but no. Park your car lady, and then we'll crack your brain open. Finally, somehow, I made it into space, and there I sat, in the car, staring at the red lights over the emergency room door. Do you ever wonder why the signs are always in bright red? Red, like blood. Who thought of that one? It could not be something like yellow. Happy like the sun. Okay, perhaps red made more sense.

God, are you listening? What do I do? Brain tumor. The words kept spinning in my head. As I walked slowly to the door, my phone rang. It was my friend, Liz, asking to make coffee plans. Coffee. I loved coffee. Caffeine. I wonder what that would do to my brain, could that have caused this? My head spun.

I am at the ER; the words spilled out. I think I'm dying. "I'm on the way," she said, and slowly, my feet started to move, heavy, and slow, I found a way to walk in the door. I told the ER clerk my name and that a brain surgeon was supposed to be waiting for me. She looked at me as if I were nuts. Guess there aren't too many of these walking in the door. There was a flurry of activity, and before I knew it, an actual brain surgeon was standing in front of me. He was talking, but all I was thinking was how civilized he seemed. Would he be the one to crack open my skull? He was soft-spoken with a southern accent. I know he was explaining my situation and the upcoming surgery to me, but all I could think about was how civilized he was. Then my mind wandered as if I wasn't present at all, wondering, what does a brain feel like? Is it mushy? Can you imagine holding someone's brain in your hands? Someone's personality, memories, capabilities? Would this be the man I would trust with my brain, my ability to think, to walk and to breathe? My entire quality of life in his hands. Did I have a choice? One step at a time, breathe. I could still breathe, that must be a good sign, right?

Then I was in a room. Wondering…why would God save me?

Breathe

The last year or so, I'd grown more introverted. My life revolved around my daughter, my work, my mother (who lived with us), and our pets. That's it. I had gotten sober 16 years earlier, but I couldn't remember the last time I'd been to a meeting. I rarely saw my friends or family, and I had stopped going to church. I'd had ankle surgery earlier in the year. My boss had given me a hard time about walking with a cane, so I'd felt insecure and worked like a maniac to hold on to my position as an executive with a Fortune 200 company – to prove that I was still 'good enough' while knowing I was already handicapped. Boy, if he was worried about me walking with a cane, what would he think of a potentially new, bald me? Would I be bald? Would I even get through the surgery? Why am I thinking of these things? Work. Baldness. None of that mattered now. Life or death, what would it be?

I just wanted to live and keep being a mother to my daughter. That's all it came down to. The rest of the world, the wants, the needs just slipped away. I sat in that cold emergency room and wondered if this was it. Just breathe, I kept telling myself, just breathe. Then I wondered, as my soul quieted, what do I do now?

Maybe this is what we should do every day just for the sake of it. Stop and in silence, ask ourselves if I were dying, what would matter? What would I care about, and what would I do next? Would I run to a loved one, play hooky with my children? Call that person you have a crush on that you think doesn't know you're alive? How many things do we push off because we believe we have more time; how would we live differently if we didn't?

Help Me, Dog!

I was in a room in the ER, and I could see patients being moved in and out by orderlies. Nurses and doctors were coming in to check on the monitors that I was hooked up to, but for the most part, I didn't know what they were doing. They talked in hushed tones, and that creeped me out, most of all. They treated me like I was a hopeless case, and this was the most exciting thing to happen in their day. I bet it was more interesting than the flu shots and broken bones they usually see. Could they make me more comfortable, they asked, was there anything they could do? Yeah, tell me this isn't real, it's just a horrific nightmare. Wake me UP!

They couldn't do that, though, and I was desperate for comfort. Something made me ask if there was a dog in the hospital. Some hospitals have therapy dogs on duty, and although I knew it was a long shot, it's all I could think of at that moment. I wanted to wrap my arms around a dog. I'd always wanted to train my dogs to do therapy work, to be of service together, but I think now, I've run out of time … time for all those plans. I couldn't understand anything that was going on. I was in a daze and the activity around me – nurses, doctors coming in and out – it was like they spoke a foreign language. It was all just faraway noise.

I'm not sure how much time went by, but there was a knock at my door, and a woman poked her head in. "You asked for a dog?" she said softly, and I must have nodded because she came into my room with a short-legged, adorable Corgi. They are the kind of dog that follows the Queen around at her castles in England. Unlike the Queen, I knew this woman – she worked at my vet, talk about a small world. Hi Kelly, can you help me with some flea medicine? Nope, not today, today I need something different. Hi Kelly, I'm the patient that's got something crushing her brain, the dying woman who asked for a dog. Considering the shock that she must have felt seeing me in such a different setting and circumstance, she recovered quickly and with incredible grace. She introduced me to her Corgi, Raider.

I was on the floor, how had that happened? Had I curled up on the floor to escape the world around me, curled up in a ball as if somehow, I could make the reality of this day drift away? Raider came closer to me, and he was all I could see. Dog! Help me! I cried in silence in my head. He looked at me with soulful brown eyes; he could see into my soul. I wrapped my arms around him and felt his warmth; everything felt still and safe for a moment. Face buried in his fur; all was right with the world for those simple, peaceful moments.

GOD, are you listening? If you are, if I survive, I promise to have a therapy dog. I wondered, was I in that stage they talk about in books, deal-making or something? Hm, am I serious or just desperate? No, I really meant it. It wasn't a 'hey if you save me, I'll do some good' it was more of an 'I always meant to, and if I survive, I promise to'… oh wait, I guess I was deal-making. I suppose in moments like these you'll do anything, say anything, for a little more time.

Dogs really can change your life. My first dog in my adult life was Logan. I was absolutely in love with him. He was a tri-colored Cavalier King Charles Spaniel with markings on his face that seemed to exaggerate his every emotion. I didn't go anywhere that he couldn't come with me. We lived in the North End of Boston together in an ancient building right behind the Old North Church. The Freedom Trail ran right by our building, and every day, thousands of tourists would walk by our front door. It was a beautiful, quiet cobblestone street surrounded by parks and gardens. We had the second floor, and Logan would sit in the quaint front window watching the tourists walk by. They'd take pictures of him and come back year after year, asking to see Logan, whose images traveled the world. I threw birthday parties for him in the park, and we made friends together. We started a crime watch together, after all, who better to watch over the neighborhood than the people who walked their dogs during the day. This wasn't the suburbs; we didn't have fenced-in yards, so we got to know our neighbors that way.

I'd always thought of training Logan to do therapy work – he was just that kind and loving. Patient with everyone he met. Well, unless you had a backpack on your back, those freaked him out, and he would growl in warning at anyone with one. In a college town, you can imagine. How many people he warned – you've got something on your back, watch out! Oh, and trench coats, perhaps I'd watched too many action movies with him curled up at my side, where the bad guys wore long black trench coats. If he saw someone with one on, his sweet personality would melt into a quietly growling one, even if it were a hundred-year-old woman trying to stay warm on a cold winters day, he'd growl up to her as if she was hiding a gun under her raincoat. Can you imagine? Usually, it was a neighborhood person commenting on how adorable he was, and just as they'd bend down to pat him, his little teeth would show in a shocking growl. They'd snatch their hand back and rush away looking over their shoulder as if the devil himself was packaged in that sweet looking dog. It didn't help that he owned his own little trench coat, hell, he had boots, a snowsuit, a Red Sox t-shirt, even an Irish knit sweater hand made by my mother.

He wasn't just the best-dressed dog in Boston, though; he was smart, super smart. When he was still a puppy, we were doing the puppy pads. I'd brought him home in the middle of winter, and the idea of going out into 3-foot snowdrifts to teach him how to 'do his business' wasn't appealing in the middle of the night, so puppy pads it was. I kept them in a bathroom out of sight, but he learned that if he went there to do what he needed to do, he was rewarded with a cookie. He was adorable; he'd sit and look at me with those soulful eyes then go running to the bathroom. I'd hear him moving around on his pads; then he'd come out, chest puffed out in pride and scamper to the kitchen and sit by the counter where the cookie jar was kept, awaiting his peanut butter treats. One day, something made me go in and check to make sure his poop was healthy or some such justifiable reason.

13

That's when I realized the pad was all wrinkled, but there was no sign of anything deserving of a cookie. He had learned how to fake me out and for weeks, had been running in there, out of sight, made a little noise as if he was doing his business, then came out proudly to be handed his prize. Now, you're probably wondering, why hadn't I figured this out sooner. Don't be mistaken; I was wondering that too.

He was more than a precious, too smart pet, though. Logan saved my life one day when he was less than a year old. We'd been taking a stroll through our neighborhood, walking towards a corner store where I'd often shopped when he started to freak out. He turned around and tried to pull me in the opposite direction towards home. I'd tried to calm him down, but to no avail; so, I gave in and scooped him up in my arms and turned to head towards our apartment building. Within moments, I heard a massive explosion, and the ground shook under us. I turned in fear to see what had caused it, and there, so close in front of us, we could feel the heat, was a tower of fire at least 50 feet high. I ran as fast as I could in the opposite direction, screaming for someone to call 911. We learned later that gas pipes had burst, and fires were burning under the streets of the North End, causing the maintenance hole to explode, shooting fire towards the sky. Logan, my hero. It was no wonder that in the years to come, I'd pampered him in every possible way and rarely was seen without him.

A few years ago, Logan had died of a brain tumor of all things. They were rare for Cavaliers. I couldn't help but wonder what a crazy coincidence. He'd saved me once. You hear the stories of dogs saving their owners, licking spots that silent cancer was growing, notifying neighbors when someone is hurt and needs help. Had he somehow given me more time, absorbed some of the killer tumor that was trying to take my life now? Had he caught it from me somehow? I know these seem like irrational thoughts, but it's not like I was rational. I missed him, my little Logan. So, God, if your listening, if I manage to survive this, I promise to have a therapy dog. To give back as I'd meant to, before.

Letting Go

My friends came to visit, bringing a pastor from my church. I'd never met him before, but he seemed familiar to me. It just goes to show how little I'd been attending church. It turned out he was the central figure in our church's worship band. I think he was the only one that didn't ask how I was doing; he just seemed to know. Pretty bad. Did I want to pray with him, let him pray for me? There is no reason for Him to save me. I whispered. We talked for a while, and as he listened to my fears, he held my hands, and in those hours, he seemed to come to know me. He believed in me. I realized that somewhere along the line, I'd stopped believing in myself. He told me that he believed God still loved me and that He wasn't done with me yet.

How could he know that, how could anyone? I don't know why, but I desperately clung to those words. I started to have a glimmer of hope. Even though a part of me realized that he probably says that to all the dying people he meets in the hospital, that's his job, right? But in those moments, I desperately needed hope, and so I needed to believe him, that somehow, he'd divined I had some value and that he had a direct line to God. My neighbors came; they brought my mother and my daughter, the center of my world, Kajal.

My mother was upset and flustered. She pointed to the bed, "Lisa, you don't want everyone to see that do you?". What, I wondered aloud? "Your weight' there's a scale in the bed, it shows your weight." I know I need to lose some weight, but now, at this moment, I'm dying, and that's what she's worried about? Someone might see my weight. I know she loves me, but I also know she truly believes I'd be embarrassed. I probably would have, at any other time in my life, been completely mortified. But now it didn't matter. All my energy was gone; I was lost again in a cloud of pain and darkness. What's next? What do I do next? I asked the nurse to turn off the scale. The room was full of people, I don't remember everything, everyone, but I remember wondering do they care? Do I? But my mother did, so I saved her the embarrassment, or what she thought was mine. It didn't matter anymore, did it?

My brother Brad was communicating with the hospital. Looking back, I could have sworn he was there with me, looking me calmly in the eyes and holding my hand. I learned later that he wasn't in the room. He'd been on the phone with me, asking me to trust him. It was what my life boiled down to. Live or die, the decisions we were about to make together would set the stage for whether I would survive. It's no wonder I thought he was there with me. It doesn't get more intense than this.

From what I understood, they had faxed him the wrong records. I guess the night before (at this point, I'd been in the hospital throughout the night), they had sent him someone else's records reflecting a brain hemorrhage. It wasn't as bad as what I'd first told him, so he had been relieved. He had first called my family with the 'bad' news, but then had received these records and called everyone back to tell them it wasn't as bad as we'd initially thought, it was 'just' a brain hemorrhage. Can you imagine, a brain hemorrhage wasn't as bad as the monster tumor I'd communicated initially to him? But as he'd read through the records, he'd realized the hospital's error and that they'd sent him the wrong patient's records. He immediately asked the hospital to send the correct ones. Realizing that the facts were, in fact, dire, he called my family back and told them the horrifying truth. The mistakes continued though, he reviewed my 'real' records and found out that the hospital hadn't put me on anti-seizure medicine, which I guess is the protocol for someone in my situation. They had put my life at further risk (could it have gotten any worse?) and my Buddhist, surfer, never frazzled brother Brad was furious and told me he didn't trust the hospital, that they couldn't save me. He was afraid if I stayed and had surgery there, I wouldn't

16

survive. He wanted to have me transported to Duke, where they had a world-class brain tumor clinic. He and my older brother, Phil, were already making the arrangements.

The neurosurgeon came in and talked with me. He told me it was a miracle I was alive. He didn't know how, with a tumor as massive as mine was, I was still functioning. The tumor was crushing my brain, and it was moving from the right side to the left, growing quickly. Breathing, walking, talking, it didn't make sense that I was still highly functioning, through all the pain and considering what was taking place in my head. It was a war zone, and the bad guys were winning. The surgeon shared that he knew my brothers were trying to send me to Duke, but he begged me not to go. He told me not only was he unsure that I could survive the four-hour ambulance ride but that if I did when the doctors saw me, they wouldn't understand how critical I was because there was simply no way someone could have a tumor as bad as mine was and still be conscious and coherent. He asked me to trust him. He was so kind; I was confused and scared. I didn't know what to do, but I believed him, so I told Brad that I should stay put and have the surgery in Charleston.

Brad told me that he'd never tried to tell me what to do in my life. He had always respected my independence, but he begged me to trust him, he believed I'd die if I stayed there, that my only hope, my best hope was at Duke. He asked me to let him take care of me. To let go of trying to control this situation, to turn over the decisions about what would happen next to both he and my older brother Phil. Phil had the connections to help me. He was an executive at one of the most successful companies in the world, and his colleagues had graduated from Duke. They were helping us. They were reaching out to a famous surgeon who headed up their brain tumor center, Dr. Friedman, who operated on Ted Kennedy.

Wasn't he dead? I wondered, but my brothers were working together to try to save me, and they believed this was my only hope. One a doctor, the other a business leader, they cared about me. Had I doubted that? Probably. Who was I anyway? I've always taken care of myself, been fiercely independent, but on that day, I didn't know what to do anymore, I was terrified of making the wrong decision, so I gave my trust to my brothers, and they made the arrangements. God, are you there? I am done trying to control everything; I'm letting go and turning it over. It's in your hands and theirs now.

17

Turning it over, sounds easy right? It's probably one of the most impossible things any of us can ever do. In a world that's always telling us we're not enough, don't have enough. We're bombarded by advertising and marketing that tells us what life should look like. We watch others on social media living seemingly perfect lives with perfect partners who love them completely, and we look at our own lives and wonder why we don't have that? Why am I doing what I'm doing? Why am I living where I live or working where I work? Is this the person I'm supposed to live with forever, or will I ever find that person, any person, to love me? We feel alone, misunderstood, unique. We hold on so tight to everything, and often we're just barely scraping by.

I had always dreamed of having a partner who would love me completely, someone who would take care of me, showering me with love and material support. I was quite superficial, thinking that jewelry and flashy cars somehow represented love and security. I went from relationship to relationship, hoping that the next time, it would be right. Geez, when I was in college, I fell head over heels for a man who I believed to be a successful real estate developer. He was quirky with a quirky sense of humor, and for some reason, I never questioned why he traveled with a pack of friends and the extreme wealth that seemed to surround him. By the time I realized the 'friends' were not friends at all, but bodyguards and the rumors started to reach me, I had blinders on and was so deeply in love, the truth couldn't touch me. I was a ridiculous romantic and refused to believe anything bad about 'my' love, especially when the rumors sounded like something from an episode of 'The Sopranos.' The truth was, I just wanted to be loved, and here was a man who loved me. I was afraid of looking too deeply. The night before he was indicted on 13 counts of racketeering, he had whispered to me, "I'm sorry hon, I'm not the angel you think I am." Seriously?

My life was either a whirlwind of romance or utter aloneness. I never imagined that I'd find completion through single parenthood, by loving a child that was born half a world away. One who looked about as different from me as you could get and spoke another language. Another language! We didn't even understand a word the other was saying for almost six months. Somehow, taking care of the bravest little child in the whole world (one who knew what starvation looked like up close, and had to figure everything out on her own for 5 ½ years) was just the magic that I'd needed to fill the hole in my heart. My joy came from loving her, giving to her...not from other more superficial and material things. Then, the rest of my life seemed to fall into place.

I became successful at work, and I held on furiously to my job, as I saw it for what it was, my primary source of income. I had been a successful recruiter for years and had a taste of some creative success when one year, I took time off from recruiting to help produce an independent film. A friend of mine from college had known about work I'd done in the nonprofit world for seriously ill children and had reached out for help with fundraising. I knew nothing about independent films or the movies, but I'd been raised that when someone asks for help, you do what you can to help them. I thought, why not? Let's make a movie. The movie had an inspirational quality for families that I was motivated by, and I threw myself into it. People thought I was nuts, who goes into independent films? But before I knew it, I was being handed a book on 'how to produce an independent film,' and I stepped into the world of executive producing. Time flew by, and our little film made it into the Sundance Film Festival, sold out there, and won the Audience Award for Best Feature Film. Celebrities courted us as we lived on hot dogs in our mountainside villa, and following that, the movie went on to win Best Feature Film at the Nantucket Film Festival.

I would have remained in the film world if I hadn't found myself quickly growing broke, so I returned to the corporate world of recruiting to keep my head above water, taking on the occasional film project on the side to keep my creative juices flowing. But fast forward a few years, and my move toward a more secure future had placed me in a position where I'd moved up the ladder into management in one of the most respected corporations in the world. I worked like a maniac at times, and I became more and more controlling as a person. As a single mother, I was the responsible one, the only parent, and I took that to heart.

My mother lived with us and helped me with Kajal, so thank goodness I wasn't completely alone, but I was fiercely protective of her and the life I'd built for us, and I'd become slow to build relationships in the outside world. I wasn't the materialistic, desperate for love woman I'd been when I was younger, looking for someone to take care of me. Somehow now, I had become an independent woman who had to give up all control and hopelessly turn the decisions that had control over my life or my death, to another.

19

There were tests, another MRI, blood work. We were waiting for the ambulance. I kept thinking, how can this be happening? It can't be real, but it was.

Saying Goodbye

I could see the fear on everyone's faces. Not Kajal, though, she seemed so calm and quiet. I talked to her. I don't remember what I said to her, but I remember what I was thinking. If these are my last words to her, I need to let her know how much I love her. How special she is, that her life can be anything she wants it to be. I was saying goodbye to her, in case I didn't make it. I felt desperation, pain, heartbreak. How can I not watch her grow up, be there to help her through her life? Was this the last time I'd see her? How would she handle it if I died? Would she still trust, still love? Sometimes it felt like we were the only two people in the world... I prayed that she wasn't left alone. My family lives throughout the country, so I wondered who would take care of her? I hadn't made appropriate plans. I didn't have a will. I asked the hospital if I could see a lawyer, but they said no, I couldn't write a will now. It wasn't legal; it was too late for some reason. Maybe with the tumor in my head, they didn't trust I knew my own mind, that I could make life-altering decisions.

I'd asked my brother Phil years ago to be her legal guardian. I know he'd see she'd be taken care of, but his children were grown now. He'd said he would take her in when his children were younger, but his life looked different now, different from what it had looked like when I asked him to make that promise. There was Holly, who I'd grown up with. Living down the street from me, we'd gone through life as soul sisters and through all the ups and downs never had a cross word between us. I knew she and her husband loved Kajal and would adopt her as their own, but I hadn't done the paperwork, made it legal. I don't remember why. I called them anyway and asked them if they would take Kajal in if I died, and they promised they would, accepting without question.

My mother was there for us, loved Kajal with all her heart, but I knew at her age, bestowing a child on her wasn't the right thing to even contemplate. She believed in Kajal; she loved us, but she was in shock too and didn't have any answers, no one did.

Everyone was rushing around and hushed at the same time. My sister had flown in, was taking care of Kajal and my mother. My neighbors/close friends were still there. I loved them like they were family. They said they would take care of our home, Kajal, our dogs, our cats, whatever we need. Oh no, my cat Serena Sundance. She had breast cancer, was so sick, and I'd already called a doctor to see about having him come to the house to put her to sleep. To sleep, why do we say that? We're killing them, even though we do it to protect them from suffering. I had not dared to go through with it; now, she'd be suffering without me.

The ambulance came for me, and I said goodbye to my family. It wasn't just 'goodbye' though was it? It was 'goodbye.' Not, I'll see you later, but in case I don't see you again, if I don't make it, goodbye. My family was planning to follow us to Duke as I was wondering, would I even survive the ride? All I kept thinking was, had I said enough to Kajal? Did she know she was the light of my life, that she could do anything she wanted, that she had worth in this world, that I'd never want to leave her for anything in the world, that I was fighting for her? Did she know that she was profoundly and truly cherished from the bottom of my soul? As I wondered if I'd said enough, celebrated her enough, I couldn't help thinking, as they put me on the gurney and I panicked, was this it? Does she know how special she is? Does she know how amazing she is and how much I loved her? That I wanted to survive, for no other reason than to keep being, her Mom.

The surgeon told me I might not survive this ride. Would I die in an ambulance with a stranger, in the middle of a highway somewhere? The EMTs started to take me away. I grabbed at one of their hands. Holding it tight, I began to cry, and I begged him to keep me alive. I told him that I was a single mother, and I told him Kajal's story. I begged him to do whatever it took to keep me breathing. Some part of me believed that if he knew our story, recognized me as more than just another patient; he might try harder to keep me alive. He hooked me up to an IV and monitors, and we started the long drive together. He told me about himself that he was a veteran, and I shared with him that I led a program to help veterans through my work. Was I trying to win him over, with all these stories and my work to help vets? With every word, would he care more, fight harder for me? We prayed together, and he promised he would keep me alive and get me to Duke safely. The time passed, praying and crying and pleading with God to give me another chance. Anything God, just please, please give me more time. I'll make it right, be a better person.

For much of my life, I'd been active in different charities, always tried to make a positive difference in the world, but these last few years, I'd barely been able to get through the days. Juggling work and motherhood there just never seemed to be enough time to give back like I used to. I'd dreamed of adopting more children. When we moved to South Carolina from Boston, trust me, that was a trip, a liberal Yankee, single mother, business executive, and bi-racial family, yikes! Southerners didn't know what to make of us; we could have been from another planet for how different we were. I built a big house with plenty of room, but life got away from me, and the dream had fallen aside as I traveled for work and barely managed to juggle my life as it was. Was God angry at me for forgetting that calling? I always felt that the house happened so smoothly that He'd guided me to it so that we had the space to adopt more children. Had I let Him down, was this the result of failing my purpose? My pastor had told me that God didn't work like that, but a part of me still wondered, was this punishment for not doing enough? Being a better person?

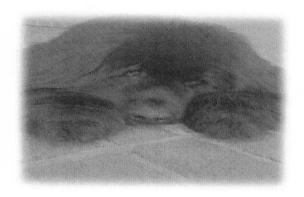

The Hospital

W e made it. We pulled into Duke, and they were waiting for us. There was so much activity around me, everyone rushing to keep me safe, but the hospital was quiet, it was the middle of the night. They took me to the ICU, and sure enough, as they wheeled me in, the nurses at the desk looked at me with surprise and told us that I must be on the wrong floor. I was conscious and talking, and to them, I looked so healthy. They couldn't see into my head, the tumor that was on the verge of taking my life, the silent killer. The surgeon in Charleston was right, I felt myself start to panic, not breathe, but then the nurses read my file and grew serious. They rushed me into a room and hooked me up to so many monitors. They explained that I was being prepped for a craniotomy. Brain surgery. Another MRI was done, and they stuck things on my head, I don't remember what they were for. They looked like large pointy metallic buttons. A team of surgeons came in to meet me; Dr. Allen Friedman was the head of brain surgery. He was quiet and kind, calm, and confident. From what I'd learned from my brothers, he was the best in the world. If anyone could save me, he could.

He introduced all the surgeons on his team. They walked me through what was coming next. They would perform a craniotomy, cut my head open, ear to ear. Then they'd peel my forehead down to the top of my nose and take off part of the front of my skull. I couldn't comprehend what they were saying; they would drill holes then saw the skull between the holes, just like connect the dots. Then they'd remove the tumor and put me back together again using screws to hold my head back in place. One surgeon's job was strictly to staple me. To place staples in from ear to ear, like a headband. He was top in his field and known for his excellent artwork in stapling to reduce long term visible scaring. They were a handsome and charming team from all over the world. They made me feel special like they cared, and I was a VIP to them. Was it because of the size of the tumor and surgeons like a challenge? I've seen that on Grey's Anatomy. Or was it because of Phil, he was the true VIP? His referral made this happen. He's one of the most respected and successful men in the high-tech world. His colleagues and boss, often seen with him on the pages of Fortune and Newsweek, were the ones who made the calls to help get me in here. I was so grateful that he'd pulled out all the stops to save my life. Whatever the reason I was grateful to be here, there was something about the team at Duke that just inspires confidence, and from what I saw, they treated all their patients as if they were the most influential people in the world.

As I reflected on my brothers and my family that was surrounding me, I thought back to my childhood. We'd been raised in a beautiful suburb just outside Boston. My parents juggled to make ends meet. My father worked as a pharmacist, and my mother, feisty as she was, ended up in politics for no other reason than to keep ensuring her children had everything they needed to get a good education. We always had what we needed, even if our clothes were often secondhand from other family members. Christmas was magical, with presents overflowing from under the Christmas tree, and we were shuttled everywhere, from the swim team to football practices. My mother was a fantastic cook, and she could make a roasted turkey last for weeks without boredom setting in. We were blessed in many ways, but most of all, that we were given the foundation of a good education, which was the springboard into successful careers for myself and my siblings.

We were all fiercely independent but knew when push came to shove, we'd be there for each other, as was happening now. We may not have lived close enough to be at each other's children's soccer games, but for us, it wasn't the day to day activities that were what knitted us together, as with other families, it was the big stuff, the 'life-changing' stuff.

When my father was living in a nursing facility a few years ago, he called me up to tell me that I would be hearing from someone from MIT regarding a program for the development of a new robot system. He didn't know much about it, but they'd visited his nursing home and asked for volunteers, and he said he would if his granddaughter Kajal could be involved. He knew Kajal was a straight-A student with an interest in robotics. They would train Kajal to drive a robot remotely to visit my father so that they could see each other and communicate across the miles. As my father's health began to decline, I'd contacted the company to make sure the program was going to kick-off, before it was too late. They scheduled their first virtual visit, and Kajal was successful in driving the robot, from an iPad in our home in South Carolina, navigating the hallways of the nursing home until it arrived at the door of my father's bedroom in Massachusetts.

When my father first saw Kajal's face projected on the 'head' of the robot, he was confused. "Kajal, I didn't know you were coming for a visit," and then he laughed when he realized she wasn't there in person, but on the computer screen. Kajal told him how she enjoyed working with the robot and that one of the program leaders was from MIT and had offered to give her a tour of the university. She thanked him for thinking of her, and his words before signing off for the day, due to being tired, was, "of course, Kajal, I love you and remember, Schillers stick together." We didn't know that would be the last time Kajal saw her Grandfather before he passed away.

That was us as a family, living distantly but crossing the miles to connect when we needed each other. We gave each other a hard time on occasion but cheered each other on too. I was always considered a bit of a flake by my older siblings; it didn't matter how successful I'd become as an adult or that I was doing a great job as a single mother. I was still the flakey blonde girl who'd been a cheerleader in high school and was oversensitive emotionally. But here they were, not just cheering me on, but seeing that Kajal was cared for and arranging for a lifesaving surgery that I'd likely not have been able to coordinate myself.

So here I am, fighting for my life and hooked up to more machines than I can make sense of. I was still thinking practically, and so I called my work, all the people that reported to me. I made sure they had what they needed to be successful in their jobs and asked them to work together during my absence. I made lists to organize what needed to be done and communicated it to each person, one by one as if I did not worry that tomorrow may never come.   Everyone was so lovely, but no one could believe what was happening. Why would they? I was in shock. I called my closest friends.

I cried with them and told them that I loved them. I was so scared, so scared of dying. I just wanted to live. All my previous worries went away. Budgets and bills, my job, and daily problems that seemed so big were gone. Nothing mattered except surviving. All I kept thinking was, just let me live. I wasn't thinking about what I could be facing if I did survive the surgery, what types of deficits I might have. That just didn't seem to matter; my mother kept whispering, just live. We can handle anything if you just live. But I couldn't help wondering, could they even save me?

It all happened too fast to process. I was in a daze and terrified in a way I'd never experienced. As they wheeled me to the operating room, each person I saw, the anesthesiologist, the surgical nurse, the surgical team. I begged each in turn, pleading with them, please save me.

Ghosts

The first thing I remembered upon waking was my dad and having coffee with him. I told him I was scared and that I had a brain tumor and was dying, but he laughed like he always did and told me he knew everything that was going on. He'd been watching over me and that he knew I was going to be ok. He told me he was proud of me and proud of my daughter. I asked him if it was my time to join him, but he told me he knew it wasn't. I had to go back, be with Kajal, live our life. There was more for me to do. It wasn't my time.

Looking back now, I don't remember waking up, but my family later shared that as I came to, I had motioned to Brad to come closer and mumbled that I had something important to share. Everyone held their breath, expecting some significant spiritual insight. I'd told him that I had a list for my sister. Lists, that was the big reveal.

It made sense. I'd been making lists for years to keep myself organized, and from the moment I'd arrived at Duke, I'd made lists for what needed to be done in my absence, to care for Kajal, our home, and pets. But seriously, my first words post-surgery was about to-do lists? No wise words for the living? No sharing about having coffee with my father, that memory was so clear and still is to this day. Perhaps at that moment, it needed to remain private, or I had a conscious enough awareness to realize they'd think I was crazy. Or maybe, very simply, when I needed to speak it was truly about what needed to be done; and I was so used to giving out directives and managing my life, Kajal's life, our household, pets, and work, that was what came to the surface of what was most important. I just couldn't drop the ball even when fighting for my life post brain surgery. Why are we all on such a life cycle of 'to do' items? Where's the living in the moment, experiencing life as it comes vs. always planning absolutely everything?

When the surgeon came in to check on me, I couldn't keep the memory of my father back and immediately told him about seeing him. But then, there was the pain. I was having trouble speaking, I couldn't think clearly, and it was hard to formulate words. My head and my mouth didn't seem to work together. At one point I was convinced there was a bear in the room, asking me questions and then, there were the ghosts. My mother, sister, and Kajal were there, comforting me and trying to make me laugh.

As dusk came, shadows and whispers started to surface. I couldn't see well, my vision was limited to some tunnel vision directly in front of my face, but out of the corners of my eyes, where I couldn't physically see, I could make out shadows rushing past, whispering. Were they trying to tell me something? Was there a reason they were in my room, or are they in all the rooms of the hospital, but not everyone could see them? I thought of the crazy tv shows where people claim to talk with the dead. I didn't take them seriously, but I'd lived in Boston, where old homes and buildings were genuinely haunted. It wasn't uncommon to experience something strange or to hear stories of things that went bump in the night.

I had had a few close calls with ghosts in the past. One Boston apartment I had lived in had a playful spirit that we came to know had a goofy sense of humor. I lived there with four roommates; the place was huge with five bedrooms, six baths, and two kitchens in over 3000 feet of converted warehouse space. Small things started happening that made us a little frightened at first, like cabinets being left open or a chair moving right before you sat in it, causing you to land on the floor. Those things we could blame on each other, thinking we were playing pranks on one another. TVs would turn on and off, and knocks were often heard on the walls. After a while, there were no more excuses, and we'd joke about the place being haunted by a friendly ghost, not feeling threatened at all, and realized that bad things only seemed to happen to one roommate who wasn't the nicest of people. A few times, she was rather nasty to me, and when she went up to her room, light fixtures would explode, sending her screaming. Although I sympathized with her fears and helped her clean up the broken glass, I couldn't help wondering if whatever was happening in the apartment was protecting me from her in some wacky way.

One day I had friends over, and I was telling them about the ghost, and of course, they laughed at me, telling me I was nuts. I happened to be playing a CD of my favorite music at the time, Andrew Lloyd Weber's 'Phantom of the Opera' (how apropos) when suddenly the music changed, and we were listening to Sonny and Cher singing 'I've got you, Babe.' I checked the CD and found that several tracks had changed to all kinds of wacky music... something that's never been explained, and at the time (it was the 90's) was impossible to do; you just couldn't record over an imprinted CD.

Another night I was alone with my current boyfriend at the time (a sexy jewelry designer from Prague) when he woke me up screaming, fire! We looked up to see a wall of flames separating us from the exit to the stairs that led outside. We threw a blanket over ourselves and ran through the fire to the wintery cold outside. Later, when a fireman asked how we'd woken up and escaped, it was the middle of the night, and he'd found there were no smoke detectors, my boyfriend told him he'd felt someone shake him awake, warning him of the fire. We both believed the 'ghost' had saved us that night as no one else was home.

The lovely North End apartment that I'd brought Kajal home from India to was a 100 plus year-old building. I had become a member of the Old North Church, which was located right behind us, and it was that tiny congregation that supported me like a family, that gave me faith in myself and God through their love and acceptance of my dream to adopt Kajal. Our apartment looked over a 17th-century garden that the church maintained, and Kajal and I had not only planted flowers there but had helped build a peace garden, a memorial to all those lost in the Afghanistan war. On the other side of the garden was an old brick building, one of the oldest in the country. One Christmas Eve, I had helped the church set up for Christmas celebrations, and as I entered the building, I'd heard a huge party going on upstairs. Music, glasses clinking, voices were talking, and laughter. The next day I'd asked the gentleman who was the caretaker (and lived in the building) if he'd had a good time. He'd looked at me stunned and told me he hadn't been home – the building had been empty. From the look on my face, he'd laughed and said simply, "you heard them too." He shared with me that he'd heard activity, talking, laughing, and singing on several occasions when no one had been present. I'd come to accept that some mysteries will never be explained and that in my mind, ghosts or spirits, whatever you might call them, do exist. But here, in my hospital room? I wasn't sure if I was losing it or if I was truly experiencing a little of what my sister and I refer to as 'Woo Woo,' something creepy that goes bump in the night.

I told the attending surgeon about the spirits, and he admitted it wasn't the first time he'd heard about them from a patient post brain surgery. He couldn't explain it. Was it a trick of the brain, all the medicine I was on or had the operation created a sixth sense? There were no clear answers.

My surgeon had told me that the surgery was a huge success, he had miraculously removed the whole tumor, and the first tests were benign. They did additional tests to confirm the diagnosis, but we wouldn't have the results for a week or two. He was so confident and optimistic, compassionate, and straightforward. I should have just taken him at his word. Still, when your head is in a pharmaceutical fog, on fire with pain and you can't think clearly for no other reason than your brain had just been released from the pressure of a massive invader, you can't exactly process information. Fear still has you in its grips as you struggle to follow the words of anyone who communicates with you. I found that just trying to focus on a person's face never mind their words was painful. Other members of the medical team had also shared it would take several weeks to see what my 'new normal' would look like, even up to eighteen months to know what I would be facing going forward truly. Someone else told me the first few days were critical; I don't remember who. I wanted to celebrate that I was alive, but it felt clear I wasn't out of the woods yet. The coming weeks would tell whether I had a future and what that future would look like. Were the ghosts a sign? Are they coming for me?

Dark vs. Light

Those days in the hospital were a blur. Some memories are clearer than others. That first night I felt like there was a war in my room. I saw, and if it's possible, I could almost feel a struggle. The darkness reached for me, fighting for me, while a light seemed to push the darkness back. It's hard to explain, but if you could imagine a wind coming towards you, strong and powerful but dark and frightening, this would just begin to capture the war that seemed to be taking place in my hospital room. Was it death, chasing me down right there in that room, or was it my brain playing tricks on me again? I couldn't tell you, but in those late hours of the night, it was real, and I was terrified. The pain was more intense than anything I'd ever experienced; my head was on fire, and sleep was not a possibility. I sat there in the darkness, feeling as if my soul, my whole being was fighting for survival. In that room where there was light, it was smaller than the dark at first, but it was growing, stronger, wrapping itself around me, protecting me.

I learned that a neighbor had shared on Facebook about my need for surgery and that she'd called on people to pray for me. Prayer requests were going out to people all over the country of all religions and denominations. My closest friends checked in with me daily, reminding me that they believed in me, that they loved me. I felt strange energy, more peaceful, and serene than you could ever imagine. Some might say it was all the medicine I was on, but I knew it wasn't that. If you could feel love, as if it were a cloud holding you, wrapping you in the warmest blanket you ever felt, that wouldn't come close to describing how I felt. The energy that radiated with love and kindness seemed to hold me. Was it God? Had He heard our prayers; did He think I was worth saving? I started to hope. Had this 'love' energy pushed back the terrifying darkness of the night before? Had it helped me survive? I began to believe that all this love, all these prayers were keeping me alive, because a part of me, down deep, knew I couldn't survive the massive assault to my brain on my own.

A member of the surgical team, Dr. Jovan, checked on me regularly. He was kind, patient, and had a sense of humor. I must have asked him the same questions over and over because I just couldn't seem to retain the answers or what was happening. He didn't seem to mind, though, and with a smile, would simply answer me and continue to explain what had happened and what I could expect in my recuperation. I felt safe and cared for. I remember him asking me questions and testing my responses. Dr. Friedman, himself, also checked in after surgery, telling me the operation had been an enormous success. The nurses in the ICU handled me with care, and my family was there for me. Everyone reassured me that everything would be okay… I had lived.

Someone had held up a mirror; I didn't recognize myself. My face was swollen, and my eyes puffy, barely open. Who was that, was it even me? My head was half shaved and wrapped in bandages, and my forehead was flat, weird. I looked like an alien. Would I ever have a regular face? Did it even matter? Geez, I remembered the days when I wouldn't leave the house without makeup. When I triple checked my outfit to make sure my rear end didn't look too big when I would see every flaw, every imperfection and allow it to reduce my self-worth, my value. Why is it that advertising, magazines, and people we don't even know can dictate the way we feel about ourselves?

Now, here I am looking at what is basically a faceless person, and all I could think about was that it didn't matter. My daughter still loved me, so did my family, my closest friends. They didn't seem to care about my blob face at all; they somehow still saw me. I wasn't the outside I realized; I was the inside. I just kept begging God to let me live, nothing else mattered.

I couldn't move very well. It was hard to lift my hand or arms; my legs didn't listen to me. Everything was heavy, and my brain didn't seem to understand or process anything. People spoke to me, but I couldn't seem to retain what they'd said. I was so confused, nothing made sense. I didn't understand what happened to me, why I was there, or what would happen next. I think I went along with everyone because I didn't know what else to do, but I kept getting confused; none of it made any sense to me. A brain tumor? How had that even happened? How could I have been walking around, living my life as if everything was normal when I had something inside of my head killing me slowly? How could I have believed life was okay only a few days ago when it was about to be blown to pieces? Now, all that mattered was surviving.

God, are you still there? You must be, I know I wouldn't still be here without you. Was it just for today, tomorrow? Would I survive the rest of this?

Slowly, some things became clear. There wasn't a bear in the room after surgery. Our newly adopted Cavalier King Charles Spaniel was named Bear, I'm assuming he was on my mind at the time I was convinced one was in the room, interviewing me. Yep, I'd genuinely believed he'd been asking me questions about how I was doing. Kajal gave me a stuffed animal; it looked like Bear. My brain had just had a little trouble processing the information and was turning things inside out. Sorting out what was real was a bit tricky. Take the ghosts; for instance, they were still there, but they only came out at dusk. I didn't have any peripheral vision, only a tiny bit of tunnel vision in front of me, but as blind as I was, I could see their shadows and hear their whispers as they rushed by, on both sides of me. There were hundreds of them; they stayed with me through the evening.

My family had been staying at a nearby hotel, and the surgeon was eager to have me leave the hospital, get away from potential infections as soon as possible. I'm guessing that having your head cut open from ear to ear leaves you a little susceptible to creepy crawlers of the viral nature. The faster I moved out, the quicker he felt my brain would heal. More importantly, he'd said that I should be up walking as soon as I could manage. That was easy to suggest, but when I walked just a few steps, I was near to collapsing. I wanted to be better, but finding the energy through the pain and disorientation was so much harder than it may have looked. I couldn't help but wonder if other patients recuperating from brain surgery bounced back faster than I was, uh oh, the competitive nature in me was surfacing.

Within days I was released to the hotel, which was remarkably close to the hospital. I had not slept since the surgery and was more than a bit shaky. Yikes! It had only been a few days since my brain was in the hands of my mighty surgeon, but here I was in a hotel making small talk with hotel employees who were kind enough not to stare at my slowly blackening eyes and swollen face. Yes, I just had brain surgery; no, the room is lovely. The words weren't coming out right; I was thinking one thing and slurring another. I got confused easily and was incredibly clumsy, struggling to walk more than a short distance.

The pain was excruciating, and sleep was still not an option. In a gift shop, I'd picked up a stuffed animal, a bear of all things. He was wearing a Duke t-shirt. Thank God for that bear. At night I couldn't put my head down, so I rested my chin on the bear, hugging it tightly. He gave me comfort when the darkness came, my family slept, and the ghosts returned. They rushed by me, crowding the hotel room. I could hear their whispers again, but the words were still lost to me. Was this what life would be like for me? Would I live in darkness with strange spirits to keep me company? Who were they, what did they want? I was in too much pain and confusion to make sense of them or to even be afraid anymore. They were just there.

A woman approached me as I sat with my family at a breakfast table. She was unimaginably brave. I knew how bad I looked, but I just didn't care. I was alive today. Bandages stretched across my head – the little hair I had left was still sticky with surgical fluid knotted together beside a swollen and bruised face. My eyes weren't completely open, and I was too weak to hold my head upright for long. She leaned closer and softly shared she was a breast cancer survivor, coming for her annual checkup. She knew a brain surgery survivor when she saw one, her friend, who now taught yoga, had survived a brain tumor. "All you have to do is focus on being at your daughter's wedding; that's your only job now," she whispered to me… "to be there, to still be there." She told me," just focus on living for that goal, one day at a time, to live for her wedding."

One day, you're making coffee worrying about work, bills, relationships, the next, a woman you don't know is reminding you to fight to live, just live, nothing else. But hanging on isn't quite as simple as it sounds.

Welcome Home

The first day home was a blur. It was only six days since the surgery, and my brain wasn't ready to process all the commotion of life moving on. Moving was almost impossible. My brain was not connecting with the rest of my body. I still looked like a Martian with my swollen featureless face, but I didn't care about that. I just kept chanting 'live, live, live' in my head. The rest was just noise.

We arrived home where friends and neighbors were waiting for us. There was so much activity; it was confusing. I was sitting on the couch; someone was passing wine. Did they know I was an alcoholic? Of course, they did; it was just a few people. My mother was toasting with them, it was a party, but the noise, it was so loud. The dogs were barking, and the sound radiated through my head, pure, white-hot pain. I couldn't take it, I wanted to scream, but I didn't want to be impolite. Excuse me, but I think my brain is going to blow up, do you mind if I don't make small talk? But I sat and smiled; I think I did, my face didn't move much, perhaps I drooled. I know that fluid was coming out of my eyes, did someone at the hospital say it was brain fluid? I think so, that's more than a little scary, am I losing memories with fluid?

My mother's best friend sat next to me, talking about how she'd never liked me. I found myself wondering if she couldn't wait to share that lovely piece of information, at least until after I knew whether I'd survive. She did seem to want to help, though, and since she knew I couldn't lie down, she offered to bring over a giant reclining chair she had for me to try sleeping on. I couldn't take change, though, and I thanked her but said no. I found some level of security, knowing that I was propped up on my couch with my animals around me. I had a path to the bathroom. I could manage with a walker, and any change was terrifying to me.

I wanted my home to stay just as it was. I couldn't process anything new, never mind things I wasn't already familiar with. The woman ignored me, insisting she knew what was best and soon ran out the door and arrived back with her husband, dragging this massive piece of furniture with them. They pushed it in the house as I frantically begged my mother to tell them "no" – take it back. As the recliner was moved into the only available space in our family room, I couldn't begin to imagine how I'd navigate around it. The neighbors dragged me from the couch, practically forcing me to 'try' it out, and my balance was so off that as I tried to sit upright on the chair, I realized it had no sides, and I was terrified I'd just roll off. At some point later, I managed to communicate with my mother that the chair had to go, and she reached out to her friends and asked them to come back and remove it.

They glared at me as they did, and I found myself thinking, oh well, you never liked me anyway. Why don't people listen to their sick friends or loved ones? Do they think that because they are sick, they are incapable of making the simplest of decisions for themselves? And why do we, when we are ill or feeling vulnerable, feel the need to be polite even in the face of our discomfort? I know that they meant well, they'd helped to clean my home (which I'm sure was no easy task considering how out of it I was in the months leading up to the diagnosis), but my voice now didn't seem to matter. But it's so hard on the people in our lives, wondering what to do, what should they not do, what do they say? Most are coming from a place of genuinely desiring to help, but not knowing how. All we can do is be gracious, say thank you, and try to be as open as we can about what we need. Even when we have no idea what that is.

Dusk came, and the ghosts were back, but I didn't want to tell anyone I was just so tired. I hadn't slept since waking up from surgery. I clung to my daughter and my neighbor Patty who was as close as a friend could ever be. She was going to help take care of me, of us, until I was able to function better. There was so much medicine; it was all so confusing. She made sense of it all and talked in hushed tones. Every noise was too loud. The only thing I could listen to without pain was Kajal playing the piano softly for me. Peaceful classical piano. My cat Serena Sundance had hung on for me; she was still alive but fighting for her life. Was it fair? No, I needed to free her and arrange for a vet to come over. Tomorrow I'll say goodbye. My sister stayed with us one more night to help us settle in. That night in the darkness, I sat awake. My sister Linda slept on the couch beside me, occasionally waking to check on me. Serena curled up in front of me, her breath started to slow, and I thought she was ready to go now that I was home.

All night, she purred, and I patted her with my clumsy hand movements. I murmured to her that I loved her, that it was okay to let go. I was in so much pain, but I wanted to give her these final moments. She seemed to rally, then fail again, but she purred all night long, and still, she lived. I was so exhausted I had trouble sitting up, but I also couldn't lie down because it was too painful for my head to touch anything, even the softest pillow. I sat, on the couch, with Serena in front of me curled up, struggling for breath, peaceful though in her final hours.

I felt something at my back and struggling to see what it was I saw our rescue one-eyed, formerly feral cat Isabella, sitting behind me, kneading my back with her paws. I immediately understood; she was trying to hold me up in her own way. She did that all night long until the morning sun came. I thought Serena would go peacefully in the night but saw it was up to me to help her pass. Patty helped me call a local vet who understood how sick I was and wanted to help us. We had to go to them, but he came out to the car since I could barely move. He took Serena from my arms and carried her into 's office to prep her for the procedure. When he brought her back to me, I swore I saw the sun glowing above her head, and when he placed her in my arms, she was purring again. I whispered to her as he gave her 'the' injection, and she purred as she passed in my arms. Welcome home!

41

Why Not Me?

My brain was healing, and I could hear it. There was a constant tapping inside my head, tap, tap, tapping. Like someone tapping on a nail, nonstop. There was also the sound of crinkling, like tinfoil being crushed repeatedly. It was so loud; there were times I couldn't hear people speaking to me over the work being done in my brain. The surgeon's nurse, Susan, was my lifeline with Duke, and she told me it was normal. She seemed to have heard it all before. She cautioned me the next few weeks would be the hardest, the most painful. I couldn't imagine it getting worse, but between all the meds I was on, the noise in my head, and the excruciating pain of my skull, I was a total basket case. She kept telling me the brain was amazing and capable of absolutely anything. As I struggled to walk, she'd reassure me the brain could relearn almost everything.

I was so weak, and a few steps with the walker would wipe me out. I would sit on the seat of a rolling walker to move about the first floor of the house if I needed to. My arms were so heavy, they were hard to move, and I couldn't write or read on paper anymore. Thanks to technology, though, I could blow up words on an iPad, super large, and struggle through making sense of them. The technology became my communication with the outside world, texting with my friends. One day I'd know a word, the next I wouldn't. Speaking was very challenging, and the words and sounds got all mixed up between my head and my mouth. When I tried to talk with friends on the phone, it was difficult not only to hear them and make sense of what they were saying but to find the words to speak back. It was exhausting and took so much mental energy that I'd be drained after just a few minutes.

I still wasn't sleeping, but the ghosts kept me company, their shadows, and whispers all around. I wished I could hear them well enough to know what they wanted, but alas, that would remain a mystery. I could tell I was hanging between life and death, fighting for survival in this ethereal, peaceful state that allowed me to battle the pain and fear. I always felt a presence with me, and my faith grew stronger by the hour. Somehow, I knew God was there in the room with me as a steady and guiding constant. My pastor came to visit, and I tried to explain, but it was hard to find the words. I hadn't been abandoned in my life of self-absorption, but more than that, He was keeping me company day and night.

I was surrounded by love. I didn't realize how loved I was. Patty and her family, her husband and children, were always there for us, showering us with love and acceptance. My church had a meal wagon going where delicious home-cooked meals were dropped by daily, so my family didn't have to live on frozen food (not that I'd done much better before getting ill).

I reflected on life, why I was still here? As I fought to live, I also struggled to relearn. Every step seemed impossible, and my balance was completely off. It was like trying to walk on a ship's deck, listing from side to side with each step. My face was still a blob, but seriously, that just didn't matter. I was so incredibly happy to be home, to be alive. We were waiting on some additional biopsies, and somewhere along the way, the results came back negative. I celebrated this positive news, but as I interacted with my family and friends, I put on a brave front. Silently I couldn't take the pain. It was brutal, hot, blinding.

Pastor Ryan stopped by again with a friend of ours from the church who headed up the children's ministry. They still hadn't given up on me, and they visited several times to see if we needed anything and to pray for my healing. I didn't have much control over my language, and when I spoke with them, I was either stuttering or talking at mock speed with no moderation over what came out of my mouth. Kajal had told me I swore a lot during that time, but I don't remember, now looking back. Thank goodness! How embarrassing! Can you imagine what I put these two through? Shocking life stories, roller-coaster emotions, and potty mouth? Yikes! If that is not a church accepting you unconditionally, I don't know what is. No wonder they prayed over me, but I have no doubt, those prayers kept me sane during those painful and very dark days.

Kajal was my constant companion. When she finally went back to school, she would put her favorite musicians (soon to be mine) on their YouTube channel, the Piano Guys, and their beautiful melodies would keep me comfortable until she came home. Our pets kept me company – Bear and Amber, our Cavaliers, our four remaining rescue cats, and Zoey, the high pitched but adorable Papillion. A rotating door of nurses, physical and occupational therapists, made their way through my daily life. I made the mistake of mentioning to one PT professional that I wasn't sure why this had happened to me, and she immediately put me on the spot by asking, why not me? Why not me? Why not any of us?

Every day we'd get up, get dressed, and think about what we had planned for the day. Someone once told me that nothing makes God laugh louder than when we plan. When we look at our calendars, think about what we have 'planned' for the day, our week, month even the coming year, do we really know? Would we live our lives differently if we could accept that we don't? Would we be happier if we found a way to live more joyfully, in the moment? Imagine this was your last day; what would you do? Who would you want to be part of it? When you stepped outside yourself and your home, what would you see? Colors seemed brighter to me; the beauty of a single butterfly was magnified. I was humbled by the different shades of green in trees, right outside my window. The earth was coming to life in a way I'd never seen it. Brighter, clearer, more colorful, and breathtaking.

Try for one moment to close out the noise of bills to pay, resentments festering, broken toilets, and the size of your hips or the fact that you are shorter than you wish you were. What do you see? Smell? Would you love differently? See it differently? In my cloud of pain, there was clarity in how

45

I experienced each moment. Beauty I never knew existed and an appreciation for all the simple gifts in my life. I appreciated the comfort of the sofa I was sleeping on (even though it was breaking down, and when you sat in one part of it you had to be careful, or you could slide to the ground), the warmth of the blanket that surrounded me and the love that lifted me.

I am sure you're sick of hearing about the pain. I would be if I were reading this and, in a way, I was, in real life. Sick of the pain. I did not want to think about it or talk about it. How are you today, someone would ask, and what would my answer be? My brain feels like it has been blown to pieces and is intensely on fire. I am a blob who can barely move, but I answered that I was ok, hanging in, getting better. The reality was, I wasn't. Getting better, that is. Without sleep (for more than a few dozing minutes at a time, 10 days and counting), I was getting a little crazy, and the pain was so unbearable I thought I could no longer function and keep living. I didn't understand what was happening. I had been told that the brain does not experience pain, but here I was in mind-bending, horrific pain beyond anything I could have imagined. On the one hand, I knew I was lucky to be alive, a miracle, so how could I complain? Perhaps the pain was a price I had to pay to be here, living.

As I sat propped up on my Duke Teddy Bear, I held my head that night. I was shaking in pain. Kajal grabbed her big brain book. Last year when we were visiting the Science Museum in Boston, she'd asked me to get it for her. Of all the cool toys and stuffed animals, my beautiful, brainy child asked for a giant book about the brain, perhaps a sign of things to come? Since I'd arrived home, we'd both used it as a reference to better understand how the brain functioned and what it looked like. Studying the book, Kajal said that she finally understood what I was going through. "Mom, you're just like Malala."

A few years ago, Kajal had to present a report in school about someone who inspired her. She had to research that person's life, then put a presentation together and dress like them. Kajal was fascinated by the brave 16-year-old who had survived being shot by the Taliban after standing up for a girl's right to education. Malala was now on the world stage, a global peacekeeper speaking on equality for girls. Malala was one of Kajal's few heroes, in the company of Martin Luther King Jr. and President Lincoln. I was in awe that she would place me in such company.

Why? I'd asked, and as Kajal pointed out in the book, she said, "she was shot in the head, and your surgeons cut into your head. The result is probably the same; you both have broken skulls". I was just glad she compared me to her hero, even if it did take a brain tumor to land in such esteemed company.

On a call with Susan, my nurse, I finally asked the question I had been dreading to ask. When will the pain get better? She asked what I meant, "wasn't it getting better already?" Nope, no such luck. It is the same. "What level is it?" she asked. The doctors and nurses always ask on a scale of 1-10, where is your pain. I often wonder how they expect us to answer, after all, don't we all experience pain differently? And what is a 5; can we have more definition, please? For example, is five getting stabbed with a knife, or is that 10, and what if I've never been stabbed with a knife? You can only rate it based on your personal experience. Please don't take this personally, but most men I know would say a stuffed-up nose is a 9.

Okay, so I answered her. On what I imagine to be a pretty tough scale where being stabbed with the sharpest electric hot knife you can imagine is a 10; I run between 9 and 12. "No," she asked, "I understand you have tough moments, but how often would you say you have them?" It's constant, I responded. Isn't that what this recovery is supposed to feel like? She was growing a little frustrated, I thought. "Let's try this another way, when does the pain come down to a 5 or 6," she asked. 5 or 6? Never, unless I misunderstand the scale. "How about a 7 or 8," she asked. Nope. "Aren't your pain meds helping at all? After you take them, the pain should reduce." No, I shared, considering I only take one every 12 hours or so. "Every 12 hours?" She practically shrieked, "You mean every 3 hours, correct?" Uh oh, I guess we'd misunderstood the medical instructions, and I'd been pretty much on Advil and Tylenol for much of the time, as I'd wanted to limit the number of narcotics I put into my body and if I took one a day it was stretching it. The nurse immediately grew concerned; even with the limited amount of pain meds, she felt there should be long stretches without high pain levels. Stay close to the phone she stated she was reaching out to my surgeon and would get back to me asap. Within minutes the phone rang, and she directed me to go to the nearest emergency room for a stat (urgent) CT scan.

I spoke with Matt, Patty's husband, and asked if he would take me. Without hesitation, he was helping me into his truck, and we were on our way. As we made polite conversation, all I could think of was 'not again.' Dear Lord, don't take me now. After all, this hell, am I dying now? I had come to believe that I wouldn't know for sure if or what my survival would look like until I'd passed the first two weeks. I was about ten days in, was I going to die now? Did God grant me a few weeks to come to terms with my life, with Kajal? Was I greedy? I'd been given this extra time to get my affairs in order, to spend more time with Kajal; was that all I could hope for? I hadn't said goodbye to her again, what was I thinking? Had I paid the electric bill? Damn, I still hadn't seen a lawyer, I should have learned! Please, please, please don't take me, God, I'm not ready. Inside I was crying, pleading, beyond terrified.

It was the ambulance all over again, but my friend Matt was in control, calmly talking to me like everything was going to be okay, like my life wasn't on the line, again. Thank you, God, for bringing friends like Matt and Patty into my life. I'd watched their children Daniel and Chloe begin their lives and grow from a celebration of their births to toddlers and now, little people with their distinct personalities. Isn't it amazing how fast babies become tiny little people with their unique characteristics? What a miracle life was. We loved them like they were our own, this is what family was, people who loved you unconditionally were there through your toughest moments and loved you the consistently. Held you when you were scared, drove you to the emergency room when you thought you were dying, just, there. Thank you, God, for every miraculous family/friend you've brought into my life.

You create your family from these friends sprinkled into your life. They don't take away from the family you're born to, but they make your life complete, from the effort you put into one another. Kajal wasn't born to me, but she grew in my heart from the moment I saw her tiny little face looking up at me from a grainy photo. She'd grown in my heart from the day God planted her in my soul through a dream of a child in a faraway country.

The Red Thread

One of our favorite storybooks that I would read to Kajal almost nightly was the story of the red thread. A fable about a King and a Queen who had a great life but were missing an essential element, they didn't have any children. A red thread started to squeeze on their hearts, causing them great pain, until they learned that to heal themselves, they had to follow it. They followed the red thread across the world until they found a child to whom it was connected. I told Kajal before she could speak English, showing her pictures and with hand motions that a similar invisible thread had joined us. I'd had to follow it to find her. One morning during the adoption process, after Kajal and I had been matched to one another, but before I'd gone to India, I'd woken up from a horrible nightmare in a panic. In the dream, Kajal was seriously ill, dying, and I couldn't reach her to give her medicine.

I was so upset that I grabbed for the photographs the adoption agency was sending me monthly and compared them in order of when I'd received them. I had studied every inch of them upon their original receipt, but now

I was looking at them in order. I wasn't sure what I was looking for until I realized Kajal appeared to be losing weight. Since I'd been sending resources in dollars to India to help support her meals, this didn't make sense. I had called the adoption agency and told them I was worried she was ill. When they asked me why I would think that, I had to share about the nightmare, and of course, they thought I was completely nuts.

I couldn't get the panic out of my mind and told them that it might sound crazy, but a dream had driven me to adopt in the first place, so as crazy a lady as they thought I was, I wasn't going to give up unless they sent a doctor to check on her. I put on what Kajal now calls my 'work voice' and would not take no for an answer. After a few days of nonstop calls, they gave up (probably just to shut me up) and sent a doctor to check on her. Ready for this? She was sick, really sick. She had active tuberculosis and had to go on an immediate course of super strong antibiotics. She could have been dead within weeks, but instead, she started to bounce back, and all was good in no time. I trusted the dream and the soul thread that seemed to connect us.

I think Matt and Patty connected to us with these God-spun threads. We were family, that is all there was to it. I had other friends the thread had brought into our lives. We think of them as family... 'friends' just doesn't capture the magnitude of who they are in our lives. Holly, whom I have known since first grade, Bill and Terry, and others that I loved so much. They were always there through ups and downs, never judging, just loving. Isn't it amazing when people love you ... really love you? Or that feeling you get from loving them? Pure and simple joy. I remember before I adopted Kajal, someone asked me if I was worried that I would not love her as much as if I'd given birth to her, as much as other parents loved their children. I had responded that the thought never occurred to me.

Before she came home from India, I was sick with worry about her – before I even knew who she was. Did she have enough food, was she being cared for in a kind manner? Was she safe and not suffering? My heart asked these questions long before I knew her name or her face. Now, I can't even think back to my life before her, I thought I was happy 'before,' but the reality is my life didn't start until she came into it. Now, I would die for her in a heartbeat. I would give her my heart without thinking twice.

Family

I love the family that I was born into. When the chips are down, we come together no matter what. But we are all off living our own lives and aren't as active in day-to-day life challenges. Isn't it interesting what we put ourselves through? We spend so much time wishing people loved us more than they did, understood us more. We want different family dynamics. We always want 'more' instead of accepting the people in our lives for who they are, instead of something or someone we need them to be. Maybe we just need to focus more on accepting that they are who they are – then we'll be free to love those who are in our lives or who may come into our lives because we freed up the space to be accepted as we are, right now. Not as who we want to be or think we need to be. Acceptance and forgiveness, how freeing those little words are. Letting go of expectations and being ok with the relationships we have in our lives. Loving our family and our friends, for exactly who they are, unconditionally accepting them. The golden rule.

My family is unique; there's no doubt, we were blessed with parents who pushed us to appreciate education and to be there for one another, even if we were as different as night and day. Those differences helped us to become the people we were meant to be.

My little brother, Brad, had decided to take a break from his college days for a trip to Taipei. There he studied Buddhism, learned to speak Mandarin, and taught English to local children. He lived there for years until coming back to the states and putting himself through medical school. My older brother Phil, I had adored for as long as I can remember. In junior high school, he found a way to make time for me, even though he was the 'cool' older brother. We would hang out in his downstairs room complete with a drum set he'd practice on while he introduced me to music appreciation by playing Phil Collins and the Who. He took me to my first high school party at one of his best friends' houses and protected me from hooligans as only a good big brother can. He'd studied oceanography and genetics but went on to lead one of the most successful computer companies in the world. He was married to a beautiful and kind woman and are parents to two brilliant and creative sons.

My oldest sister, Linda, was the practical one, beautiful and strong, and the backbone of our five siblings. She'd been successful academically, earning a master's in education and had risen through the ranks of a Massachusetts school system. Her husband was a retired ironworker who'd climbed some of the tallest buildings in Boston. They had two sons who were not just my Godchildren, but two of the most loyal and loving sons anyone could ask for. One had served our country in the Coast Guard, and now they both lived lives of brave service as state troopers. My littlest sister, Lizzie, had experienced some heartbreaks in life but remained true to her creative self and would likely one day be a published poet. She has three children and may very well be the most sensitive of us all. She lived in Florida and hadn't been able to make it up for my surgery but was there in spirit, calling daily to make sure I knew she loved me and was praying for me.

When life is at risk, it is incredible how your mind wanders, what becomes important, and what you realize isn't. How clear everything appears and how peaceful you become. How simple everything is and how easily the answers to the big questions become. But life being at risk is one thing and being ready to leave another. I was not prepared to leave. I knew, Kajal still needed me.

When she first came home from India, I had come to realize the horrors she had survived there. She had lived on the streets, alone as a toddler, and ended up in a horrific orphanage. She did not know what it was to be cared for or even 'liked' by another human being, and she didn't know what it meant to feel safe or know that hunger would be answered with regular meals. I'd remembered that if I could give her one gift only, beyond a safe and nurturing haven, it would be a sense of self-worth. A knowledge that in her core, she was of value.

For the first five years, we were together; she hadn't trusted that if she did something wrong (in her eyes), she wouldn't be sent back to India. They say that it takes as long as they were on their own following the loss/abandonment of their birth family before an adopted child feels genuinely 'safe' and accepts their family is now 'forever.' I'd tried many things to help build her self-confidence. From role-playing how to handle bullies in school to decorating a magical bedroom and singing songs about her beautiful brown skin, to giving her flight lessons when she was only eight years old. I constantly reassured her that if she tries her best in school or athletics, then she was successful in my eyes. I wanted her to know that she could be that she was truly worthy of being loved and having a good life.

Maybe it was just ego speaking, but I honestly did not think we were done with each other yet. I believed to my core that she still needed me. I pleaded once again, God, please don't take me yet.

Your Village

There's this new term, framily, that defines people that have been brought into your life, I like to think by God vs. just by accident or some weird turn of fate. They start as acquaintances, become friends, and eventually, they become an extension of your family. They're the family you choose through shared life experience, trust, and reliance that builds up over time until you reach a point where you can't imagine your life without them. Take my neighbors Matt and Patty, for example. I couldn't have survived the last few weeks without them. I thought back to when we'd first met. We had both just moved into houses across the street from each other, in a new community with streets still bare of homes. Somehow, before they'd moved in, I'd learned they had been robbed. Patty was pregnant, and her family had thrown her a baby shower. They had moved all the baby's new gifts into the nursery. Someone had kicked in their door and taken every gift, every little teddy bear and piece of baby clothing. My heart had broken for them, sickened that they could be so violated at a time that should have been so joyful. I didn't know them yet, but I'd put the word out to some families I knew with younger children, and before I knew it, I had a few bags of baby clothes. I knocked on her door and asked her if they would be open to our help. I offered to hold a baby shower for her and invite some neighbors to help restore some of the stolen gifts.

She must have thought I was some loony, busybody neighbor, but she accepted, and so our friendship began. She was reserved and quiet when I first met her, but she didn't turn me away. Soon after she'd given birth, Christmas eve arrived. My dogs were barking at something outside, and when I looked, I saw a van backed up to a house a few doors down from me. Some shady-looking characters were loading a refrigerator into the back of the van.

The neighborhood had been made aware that there was a group of thieves robbing our community. As new homes were built, they were getting hit before the new homeowners even had a chance to move in. We had our washer and dryer stolen right out of our garage, where some subcontractors had left them before our closing. I don't know what came over me, but fury took over. Kajal, keep the dogs in the house and call 911! I didn't think twice. I ran towards the house, screaming at the men as they lifted a dryer into the van. "GET OUT OF OUR NEIGHBORHOOD! LEAVE US ALONE! THIS IS OUR NEIGHBORHOOD! NOT YOURS! DROP THAT DRYER RIGHT NOW!"

And what do you know? They dropped the dryer and took off driving at full speed through the cul-de-sac with the van doors swinging open. Patty's father ran outside to see what was going on, and they were calling the police too. By the time the thieves reached the entrance of our neighborhood, the sheriff was waiting and blocking the street. The van crashed on to someone's lawn. The criminals took off on foot, and a chase ensued through nearby woods with search dogs and everything! They caught the men, and as far as we knew, they'd been arrested.

I remember shaking afterward as the Sheriff interviewed me. "Ma'am, that was very brave, but please don't do that again. They were armed and could have pulled a knife or gun on you, just don't do that again." I was shaking, realizing how crazy I'd been. I had not even thought; I was just so mad thinking about how they had stolen a new mother's only baby supplies. Even though I didn't know her, it had broken my heart, and I'd become fiercely protective of her. This was my first house, I'd built it working closely with the builder through the selecting of every door, cabinet and light fixture, and this little neighborhood suddenly had represented all my dreams for a family and a future. No one was going to mess with that. And so, from the criminal acts of others, a friendship was born, and now here we were six years later, and these same neighbors were my beloved friends who were helping me through a battle, not for our homes but for my life.

I found myself thinking about how many opportunities pass us by? When I thought back on my life, all the good stuff, the great gifts, I could track back to helping someone else. Stepping up when someone is in need. My mother always taught me to give back. To open your home if someone needs a place to stay. On holidays she believed in an open-door policy if someone had nowhere to go, they were welcomed at our house. She felt the same way about animals. If an animal appeared lost, my mother would bring it home and voila, we had a new pet. Of course, that was before leash laws, so we had a few angry neighbors. Everyone came to know that if their dog or cat didn't return home, just knock on the Schillers' door, and hopefully, there they would be. Even the bad stuff that happens, when you look back, you realize that the bad brought something good if you just keep showing up. I used to wonder, as many of us do, why God lets the bad happen at all? A pastor once told me, it's not that He makes the bad happen, it just does. That's living. But if you have faith, you can come to believe that He'll take all the bad and turn it into something good.

In my sobriety program meetings, they will tell you, just keep showing up until the miracle happens. People with a lot of sobriety tell you they are grateful for their alcoholism. I never believed that, and it used to make me furious to hear. How ridiculous! How could I possibly ever be thankful for a disease that makes it impossible for me to enjoy an alcoholic drink? Even now, you know how much I'd like a glass of wine? Champagne? But for me, it was never just one glass, so no, that wasn't an option for me. Years into the program, I began to understand just what other alcoholics were trying to tell me. I became grateful for my alcoholism, grateful for the program that gave me tools for sobriety and daily living. Thankful for the incredible friendships the program and sobriety brought to me. The message of service, how, when you are feeling low, remember, there is always someone else lower. Reach out to help that person, then see how fast you forget your problems.

57

If not for all my broken relationships and painful breakups, I wouldn't have become a single mother to the most magical child on earth. Now this child wants to become a doctor, a surgeon. Imagine the lives she'll help moving forward? We'd made a deal. She could never become so successful that she'd forget to give back. She committed that she would one day operate on those who couldn't afford it. Perhaps children who need their medical miracles. My gift of love will be passed on to others through her in the future. What a legacy that is! Here I had wondered if I could help this precious child develop a sense of self-worth. She had survived such a brutal first five years in India and came home to me with zero understanding of who she was or who she could be. Being loved was a new experience for her, never mind being cared for and cherished.

Now, look at her, talented beyond belief. She could play the cello and the piano. She Aced her way through honors classes and was a top student in her school. She believed in herself more than any teenager I had ever met, defining her style and her dreams. Thank you, God, for guiding me along this path to be there in the best way for her.

I remembered years of granting wishes for seriously ill children and the joy it brought to me even though it was excruciating to see children and their families suffering. I felt blessed by being in the presence of such strong souls. The families used to tell me that the wishes we had granted had brought joy back into their lives at a time when no joy seemed to exist. I was sure that if I thought back carefully, every good thing in my life could be traced back to either helping another person or a painful experience in my life. Helping others and hanging in through tough times. Perhaps that was the key to living, to life.

Ok, I'm sorry, the last thing I want to do is become melancholy or lecture, but in these crazy intense times when the pain of starts to suffocate you, that's when your mind starts to wander, and the 'big' questions creep in, why is life one massive rollercoaster?

Pain Relief

So back to the present. My head was on fire, the pain so horrific I could barely move. I wanted to scream and to cry out; I can't take this anymore! But that wasn't an option; I had to keep it together for my family. My neighbor Matt had driven me to the emergency room, and he dropped me at the front entrance (to try and find parking himself, geez what is it with hospital entrances and the lack of parking spots?!). I struggled through the crowded waiting area of the emergency room. It was packed with drunks and people high on drugs, sick and broken, filling every seat. It was standing room only. I approached the front desk, leaning on my walker, and before I could formulate a word, the 'receptionist' pointed me to a computer screen. "Fill out the form on the computer, then take a seat," he said gruffly.

My head was still bandaged from surgery, and I was trying to stand without collapsing to the floor. I told him I just had brain surgery and wasn't sure I could read. The words weren't coming out right – that my surgeon needed an emergency brain scan. I handed him my surgeon's number to call, but he kept pointing me to the computer. I had seriously thought I'd told him it was an emergency. I could be having a stroke or brain hemorrhage, but he just kept pointing to the computer. I could not see the screen well, and the letters were jumping around. I wasn't sure how to type, but I knew I'd managed on my iPad. It was the only way I had kept in touch with my friends. It was painful trying to focus, concentrating on each word even with my fingers that didn't always connect with my brain.

Matt came back and helped me with the computer; then, he found seats for us. We sat next to a drunk family with the flu. A child sprawled across a few seats wrapped in a blanket; she was coughing and running a fever. Her mother was laughing with friends. She was high or drunk, I couldn't tell, but her friends were on the same thing, and they all joked about how sick they all were. Falling down, the drunks and addicts came into the emergency room, bleeding from here or there and managing better than I did with the computer registration process. I felt so bad for the little girl, but I couldn't move to comfort her. I wondered if my surgeon wanted me to leave the hospital to avoid infection, what would he think of me sitting here, next to the drunken flu family?

Time went by, a few hours, I thought, when finally I was escorted to the back room. Matt reassured me he'd be there for me, whatever I needed, waiting outside. But here I was alone again, inside a hospital wondering, am I dying? Has something gone wrong? Please, God, let me live. I'm not ready to die, but I can't take this pain, what is happening?

My mother was at home, taking care of Kajal. Patty was taking care of them. What a miracle that was, you go it alone in daily living, then out of nowhere, these incredible people pop into your life. If you're lucky enough to grab on and nurture those relationships, they turn into the kind of people who will walk you through your darkest and most joyful days. We just need to reach out and grab on to them, take the chance, and put yourself out there. Love others and believe it comes back to you seven-fold.

After I don't know how many hours, I settled into an ER cubicle, and a nurse came in to see me. I tried to explain that my surgeon had requested an emergency CT scan, but the nurse was confused as this wasn't something they came across regularly, so she told me she'd call my surgeon's office to confirm what testing was required. She had some trouble getting in touch with them, though, and it took a few more hours before she came rushing back in with a transport gurney to take me for the test. She was taking things a bit more seriously, so I was guessing she had spoken with Duke. She now asked questions in hushed tones and would not look me in the eye. Great.

Tears were streaming down my face from a combination of fear and agony. My head was on fire. I screamed out in pain when the radiology nurse tried to cram my head into a cage. I told her I had 55 staples and a recently cut open head, and every inch of my head was beyond the capability of feeling any type of touch. As she managed to close the cage around me, out of desperation, my mind reached for God and music. Music calmed me -- soft music, Kajal's piano playing, or the Piano Guys. A cello's low notes massaged my brain as I began to imagine Rachel Platen's 'Fight Song.' A close friend had shared it with me recently, and the words came to me at that moment. I just played it over and over in my head, praying for life as the words helped me gain some semblance of hope... 'this is my fight song, take back my life song, prove I'm alright song... this is my fight song'.

Back in the emergency room, a doctor finally came in to see me – a 'Grey's Anatomy' drop dead (I hope not) gorgeous doctor. Wavy dark hair, dark eyes, my very own McDreamy. Was he married? See, bad stuff happens, and Mr. Beautiful walks in the door. Geez, what was I thinking?

I was trying to hear what he was saying, tear myself away from that sympathetic smile on those perfect lips. Ok, so I was still alive. He told me that the CT scan showed small bleeds around my skull, where it had been sawed open. Where the new screws were, typically, the types of brain bleed would be severe, but with me, it was part of the healing process. There was also swelling brain swelling, and the combination explained the excruciating pain I was feeling.

He explained that he had seen gunshot wounds to the head that were less traumatic than what my skull was experiencing. Wow, Kajal was right! Her Malala analogy was on the mark, how awesome was she? As he talked, he referred to the fact that he had reviewed my original scans from Charleston and Duke and what a miracle I was, how close to death. He could not believe it. He talked of how the tumor had shifted in the 12 hours between my first CT scan and the next MRI. That it had moved from the right side to the left side of my brain, pushing my brain further into the stem. It was literally in the act of killing me when I walked into that first emergency room.

He seemed to be in awe. When he learned I was sober for 16 years; he understood I would want to hold back on the heavy drugs because of my fear of growing a dependency. 'Lisa, this is what these drugs were made for, situations like yours. This kind of pain can kill you'. When I shared my confusion over my knowledge that the brain did not experience pain, he

61

explained to me that the pain was coming from everything around the brain. The tumor sat on my brain for so long; we didn't know what damage was done to the surrounding area. Never mind the nerves that were cut by the large incision and holes drilled into my skull. All of that combined was enough damage to my head internally that it justified the levels of pain I was experiencing. Then he did not give me a choice but just hooked me up to an IV and explained he was putting me on a morphine drip. As he was about to push the plunger down on the syringe, he simply said, 'wait for it' and smiled… ah, that beautiful smile. Then, the morphine kicked in, oh, so this is what a five feels like (on the pain scale, silly).

We spent a while chatting about sobriety, and I tried to share what little wisdom I could with him, considering I was high on drugs, talk about irony. I kept noticing him look at me, then cringe and look away. I mean, I knew I looked terrible… a woman is never at her best with her head in 10-day old bandages, her face swollen like an alien, but cringe? Even I didn't think I deserved that. I couldn't take it anymore. I finally came straight out and asked, "Doc, do you realize that every time you look at me, you cringe with disgust and turn away?"

"Oh, I'm so sorry, I can't believe it shows that much, I was trying to hide it." Yikes! I thought, hide what? Disgust at how I looked?

"No, he stated, it's not that, you're beautiful!" … now we're talking. "Every time I look at you, I imagine what they did to you. How they cut into your skull, removed the tumor sitting on your brain. How extensive the surgery was, and I just can't handle it". He laughed. "I could never be a brain surgeon; I'm fine right here in the ER." Doc McDreamy leaned over and, in that perfect deep voice, told me to stick with my meds as prescribed, and he wished me luck. Somewhere in the conversation, I had found out he was in a long-term relationship, even in the state I was in, I wasn't that dense. I had to ask the question.

All I kept thinking was, thank you. Thank you for keeping me here and not bringing me home to you yet, God. I was so full of joy to be having another chance, and the morphine was still working its magic, so the pain was softened and dull.

My surgeon had grabbed my head at one checkup and laughed because I could not feel his hands. He'd told me that I'd never feel the top and back of my head again (I'm guessing because of all the nerves and muscles he'd cut through), and I'd felt nothing was a loss as long as I was alive, but I couldn't help wondering how I could feel so much pain when my head was numb to even the lightest touch.

Brain Power

Thank goodness for proper health insurance because, without it, I am not sure that I would have come back the way I have. Every day I had in-home health care with physical therapists, occupational therapists, nurses, home health aides. I was learning to walk again, talk (words still came out with a struggle and not always what I intended), read, and write. I couldn't sign my name or make out letters in the alphabet. I did word find puzzles and worked through baby books to relearn how to read and recognize words. It was strange I could read on a computer if I made the print large and I could type, slowly, but I could do it. I just did not have the coordination to handwrite even my name and reading on paper was more challenging.

I had a hard time focusing and computing even the smallest math problem. My short-term memory was affected, and my mother and Kajal had an excessive amount of patience with me as I forgot almost everything, they told me. One benefit was that I had forgotten the plot of nearly every TV show or movie I'd seen, so Kajal and I could re-watch her favorites, and they were like new. I had always hated to re-watch a story I already knew the ending to, but not anymore; I couldn't remember any conclusions. See small gifts.

One day working with the physical therapist, I was trying to raise my arm a few inches off a table where it lay. If I didn't think about it, it could move, silently listening to a language, only my brain seemed to understand. The trick was, learning how to do it consciously; it was as if I became paralyzed when I thought about doing something. The challenge was doing things because I wanted to, connecting my brain's desire to do something with the actual word or action. I kept staring at my hand, wanting to raise it, willing it to move until finally, it came up off the table. It was shaking and weak but worthy of celebration. I didn't feel like celebrating. I was confused and overwhelmed with sadness. Was this going to be my new life – the life I'm supposed to be grateful for? I knew in my heart I was grateful, but facing a life full-on was terrifying when I had to reteach my brain to communicate with something as simple as my hand.

How would I climb this mountain every minute of every day, how would I find my way back to the full life I thought I'd been living? I laughed out loud when I realized the miracle was that I was here at this moment and that my brain could relearn something as simple as moving my hand. The PT laughed with me, "Great work!" she exclaimed. "The brain is an amazing organ, it powers every inch of your body, and it has been proven throughout history to have incredible restorative powers, it can re-learn almost anything." She then explained how the tumor and the surgery had interrupted so many signals. The tumor had likely been sitting on a large surface of my brain for an exceptionally long time, years, and that pressure damaged the brain's surface. The surgery, too, was so traumatic to my head and brain, so massive, that it created its impact. There was no way to know what long-term damage I'd have, but slowly, day by day, I began to learn what my capabilities would be. I just needed to find a way not to let the fear cripple me, the fear of the unknown, the fear of what I could or couldn't do. I needed to learn to celebrate every tiny victory.

Thinking back to the question, my PT had asked me, why not me? I wondered again about that statement. How we go about our lives listening to horrific things on the daily news, often we just hear it as background noise without any connection or emotion to the person the tragedy happened to, or their families. Why not me? Why not you? Why not any of us, any day? We start with our morning routines thinking this day is going to be like any other. For me, it was making coffee, trying to catch my breath. Thinking that day was going to be normal. If we didn't know ahead of time what the day would hold, would we live differently? Would we call someone we hadn't talked to in forever, would we forgive or apologize? This experience was teaching me to think of every day as my last. I looked at my hand and willed it to raise; it did, a little more this time.

I was watching my brain learn something 'new.' From not connecting with my hand/arm to accomplishing the act by merely focusing on what I wanted to do. If I could re-teach my brain how to communicate with my arms and legs, imagine the possibilities.

We go through life, thinking we have limitations. We struggle because of the way we have learned to believe. I can't lose weight; I can't get good grades, I can't get a better job. I can't; I can't, I can't, but what if, just think about it for a minute. What IF you could do almost anything you put your brain to? If we started to believe that we 'could' get healthy, we 'could' get straight A's or achieve greater financial freedoms, what are our actual limitations? Perhaps a spine is broken, and you may never walk again, but could you write? Love, learn, teach? What about our expectations of other limitations? What about the day to day challenges? What if we started to approach everything as if we 'could' accomplish it and be willing to put our mind into learning whatever it was that we wanted to learn?

I did learn to walk again without a walker. In a follow-up appointment with my surgeon, he diagnosed a sinus and inner ear infection that was messing with my balance. Seriously? I'd wondered if the tumor had robbed me of my ability to manage walking, and all it took was a few antibiotics, and I no longer felt like I was walking on the deck of a ship in a storm.

Dr. Friedman had figured it out in a few minutes. He saw me struggling to walk and had told me that the part of my brain where the tumor had been, had nothing to do with balance. A quick look in my ears and boom! All I needed was a prescription, and my lack of balance was corrected. I just needed to increase my strength and coordination. I still mess up words and stutter occasionally and have challenges with short term memory, but I had developed tools to help me manage throughout the day. In moments of non-perfection, when the wrong word popped out of my mouth, those around me enjoy a humorous moment. I don't mind them laughing at my quirks.

I've learned to laugh at myself, right along with them. When granting wishes in Boston, doctors who specialized in mind over body, which also is known as psychoneuroimmunology, had told me that love and laughter healed. I believed it, who doesn't feel better when they are laughing.

True Colors

I do genuinely believe that in life, God makes good out of bad. I know I've already shared that, but I still struggle with understanding what good comes from the loss or illness of a child. That's unimaginable. But for most everything else, I can almost always look back at something terrible that happened in my life and see the good that came out of it.

I'm sure you've heard this statement a million times in your life, but you're about to hear it again. When times are tough, you learn who your friends are. You learn people's true colors. For example, in the company I worked for, I was one of a small leadership team that helped build the organization from a 50-person company into a 700-plus global workforce. We literally had become number one in the world in our area of expertise, and if I'm not humble, I can state clearly, I was a significant part of that. I'd been referred to as a global thought leader in our industry and often consulted with top executives from some of the world's top companies and organizations. I had a small leadership team that reported to me and about 150 employees, depending on the number of clients I had at any given time. I approached the business as 'treat everyone as you'd wish to be treated' and strive to make sure that everyone on my team was always treated with respect and lived a balanced life. I coached and mentored my team and truly cared about them as individuals. I poured myself into them to help them achieve their own goals and thought of them as family. I protected them through hard times and encouraged them when they doubted themselves. I loved them as I did anyone close in my life.

Within days of arriving home from the hospital, a few members of my work team started reaching out to me in concern. They shared with me that one of my most trusted lieutenants, was saying things to my team and other leaders, including my boss, that seemed to be undercutting me. She was discrediting me, saying horrible things about me, untrue things. I was at a loss. I was exhausted, in pain, and still wondering if I would survive, and here was someone I'd loved, cared for, nurtured, and mentored, and instead of supporting me in my recovery, she was playing both sides. I had encouraged her from the hospital, that this was an excellent opportunity to step up and take on more responsibility. But here she was instead, positioning herself to take over my position long term, through dishonesty and manipulation. I'd known this person was always a bit competitive and very focused on her career, but I'd also trusted her. We had shared our feelings of mutual faith in moments of personal conversation, and I was nurturing her for future leadership opportunities. But she did not want to wait, I guess; she saw my illness as an opportunity that she wasn't going to waste. My heart hurt; I felt confused and betrayed. Like I did not have enough to deal with?

My boss and his boss had all assured me I had nothing to worry about, but I could hear their confidence in me being chipped away. They liked this person who was attacking my abilities –but of course, they did, I'd always spoken highly of her, built her up. Why wouldn't they believe her when I didn't have the energy to fight back. Why do people do this to one another, especially women? Shouldn't we be rallying together, supporting one another? There were many people on my team, quite a few I had mentored over the years, and many were terrific, but unfortunately, others had blinders on, so focused on climbing the corporate ladder at any cost. My illness was a chance for them to get ahead. That's the way it was in corporate America. I did not have the stomach for it, and right now, I certainly didn't have the strength.

So here I am, fighting for my life, and I've got someone I'd managed and supported for years trying to take my job, not one-week post-surgery. Yikes! What kind of person does this? I felt threatened. As a single mother and the only source of income for my family, I became stressed at the idea of losing my position, but even more, I was deeply hurt. I started wondering if I was paranoid, letting insecurity guide my thoughts and getting caught up in the negative drama. In time though, the facts came out, and I learned that this individual had a field day taking credit for work I'd done and had no problem dishonestly discrediting my management abilities to pave the way for her career progression. She'd even called me one-day after surgery and suggested that I not return to work, stating that perhaps the tumor was a gift and that God may have another plan for me. Seriously? Was she using my faith to help her ambitions? Maybe she was right, but there was no doubt this advice wasn't coming from a Godly place. I wasn't perfect; I'd made my mistakes, who hasn't? She had been a person who had wanted to learn from me, and I'd been happy to teach. Now the student wanted to be rid of the teacher, and there was little I could do. She'd worked hard to damage my reputation, and even though I'd tried to believe that everything would work out, I finally had to accept that some things are just out of our control. We can't control how others behave; we can only do the right thing, ourselves.

I kept telling myself as long as I lived, that was all that mattered. The rest I could deal with, but boy, it was tough. I saw the darkest sides of people, but I also saw the best. No matter how much I tried to zero in on the good, the negative behavior caused me a tremendous amount of stress at a time when I should have been focused simply on survival. I had to force myself to trust that there was a reason this was all happening. After all, good always comes from bad, doesn't it?

Mindfulness

At first, I didn't have any taste buds; my brain had to relearn how to recognize tastes and smells. Would you believe the first thing I could smell was wine? Talk about messing with your mind, here I am an alcoholic, and the only thing I seemed to be able to smell was the glass of wine that someone was drinking near me. Just what I needed, temptation at my weakest moment, but thank God, I was able to resist begging for a glass, as delicious as the fragrant smell was. That's all I need to start drinking again when I was barely able to function as it was. I began to eat with tiny sandwiches to get whatever nutrition I could squeeze in. Thank goodness for those little Hawaiian bread rolls! I could manage to put the sliced turkey on them and nibble on them to offset the strength of the medicine I was taking throughout the day.

My church and a group from work had meals delivered to my home so that I didn't need to worry about feeding my family. What a gift this was. The meals were ready-made, and many came with heartfelt cards full of good wishes from many I didn't even know. It was so hard accepting help

73

from those I knew and strangers, but I didn't have a choice. There was simply no way I could have managed otherwise. The meals so thoughtful, made with love. There were gorgeous casseroles and soups, with homemade bread and desserts. I was beyond touched at the thoughtfulness of those I knew, many I hardly knew, and even some strangers who just had open hearts and a willingness to make a positive difference in the life of someone who needed nurturing.

It was a good three weeks before I finally started to doze off and capture my first few hours of sleep. Talk about appreciating the little things. Just knowing I could put my head down and sleep for ten or twenty minutes was the greatest gift.

One of my favorite books I'd ever read was 'The Miracle of Mindfulness; An Introduction to the Practice of Meditation' by Thich Nhat Hanh. I'd read it when I first got sober, as I was desperately trying to learn how to be still for even a few minutes every day. In one chapter, he spoke of being mindful of something as simple as washing the dishes, where he teaches you how to appreciate even the smallest activity in your day, and through that, learn to have gratitude and be present in every moment of your life.

What I took away from the book was to use the activity of washing dishes to center myself. To be mindful of the moment I'm in. I stand at the counter and run the warm water. I put the dishes in, then the soap. I consciously feel the hot clean water and allow myself to celebrate that I have access to water when many people throughout the world do not. I feel my shoulders, my hands, my feet, and I hold in gratitude that my hands work, that my feet and back are strong enough and capable enough to keep me upright. I feel the soap and dishes as I wash them, grateful that I have the resources to have such luxuries.

This small exercise gave me the ability to stop the noise in my head, all the lists and all the things that take up space in my mind. This practice focuses on my breath, and my thoughts solidify at the moment. The process of being grateful for simple things brings gratitude for all things, my child, my home, my health as it is, and I always walk away (or limp in this case) joyful and at peace. It's an exercise that works for me, but everyone should find what works for them. The vital thing to remember is that when you find time in your day to center yourself and be present in the moment, grateful for even the smallest item in your life, then your mind can't be crowded with resentments, anger, fear or insecurity. Peace pushes it away.

As I stumbled through my recovery, I started to notice that our dog Bear wasn't well, and we took him to an emergency vet who notified us he needed emergency surgery. He wasn't eating or walking. Bear was beautiful, outside and in. He had huge soulful eyes, and from the moment we met him, we were in love. He was referred to us after I'd filled out an application to help foster dogs for the Cavalier King Charles Rescue Club. He was larger than most Cavaliers, and other 'Cavalier' people didn't want him for that reason. Someone had dumped him in a schoolyard. What is wrong with people? When he was introduced to us, we were amazed at his silent kindness – his desperate need for affection and willingness to trust us and bond immediately. He had climbed up onto Kajal's lap, dug his nose in so deep she felt he'd connected with her ribs, and we knew we were lost. A failed foster it's called when someone takes in a foster then adopts them. That doesn't sound like failure to me, that sounds like success.

We loved this little dog. Following the surgery, Bear bounced back, and we thought we were in the clear. Then he took a turn for the worse. In a matter of weeks, we found out he had an aggressive form of cancer, and the kindest thing we could do was to put him to rest. We had only adopted him six months ago, and he was truly the best pet and friend. He was gentle and loving, soulful, and playful. I made that painful decision and held him in my arms as he passed quietly in our vet's office. I thought for a moment he had looked up at me in desperation, knowing what was coming and the guilt plagued me, but my mother kept reassuring me that I had kept him from further suffering. It seemed like in only a year, I had lost my father and my beloved pets Logan, Serena, and now, Bear. It was too much loss. That and I had been walking around with a killer brain tumor.

The first month was horrific, but with all the pain and in the darkness of night, I had felt a light. A presence of God, that was incredibly powerful. It was dark and light, suffering, and love. I tried to explain it to people – in a weird way; this was the worst time of my life and the best at the same time. I had never felt closer to God, more convinced of his presence in my life. He was just there. It wasn't that I knew I'd survive; it was that I knew I'd be okay. However, I came out of it.

Most people do not have the opportunity to sit in on their funeral. To see and hear the love that existed in their life. Being the fiercely independent single mom that I was, I rarely relied on anyone. My mother, on occasion, was that safe place. I could admit my fears and share my financial insecurities. She had my back in the early days when I could not manage to scrape it together before I'd found success in corporate America.

I had a few very close friends; they were there for me no matter what. I knew that and never questioned it even though I couldn't manage to ask for help when I needed it. Pride was my enemy. Now, in my recovery, I was forced to ask for help. To lean on people, and accept what they offered. Neighbors and friends offered to take Kajal fun places for the day, to get her out of the 'sick' ward. That was my biggest fear that she would get lost in my pain and suffering.

Kajal had missed school for several weeks, between being at the hospital and afterward. When I sat awake during the long nights for those early weeks, she was there, stretched out on the couch next to me. She helped me to the bathroom and picked my clothes out every day. She brought me food and water for medication. She never complained, never groaned that teenager groan, didn't even roll her eyes. After a few weeks, it hit me, what on earth had she experienced during this? It must have been horrifying for her. I had been terrified she would lose me, what had she felt or experienced? In a moment of quiet, I asked her what it had been like for her.

She laughed a not so happy laugh and shared that people talked around her as if she did not even exist. They spoke in whispers loud enough for her to hear, they took frantic calls and spoke of my critical illness. They talked with one another about their fears of my dying, and there she was, the child, ignored and overlooked. She was well cared for, always safe, just ignored. It broke my heart and pissed me off that my family never thought to talk 'with her.' Then I backed up and realized that they must have been lost in their fear, incapable of thinking of hers.

She said to me, "Mom, it is all right. I was never afraid. I knew you were going to be fine." There I was, still not knowing if I would make it…live through this … and my daughter was stating without any worry or emotion, that she knew I'd be okay. How? I asked. How could you have known that, when even I didn't know it, nobody did? She looked me straight in the eyes and said, "Although we don't talk about God and all that stuff all the time, I just knew Mom. I knew that my mother loved God, and he loved her and that there was no way he was going to separate us."

Just like that, my beautiful, smart, funny teenager confirmed with me the thing I was never quite sure of, that she had faith. Pure and absolute faith.

She knew how to live in the moment, how to trust blindly and believe that everything would be okay.

So back to the funeral concept. Haven't you ever wondered what would happen? To see who showed up and what people had to say? To see if anyone showed up at all? What would your life mean, when push came to shove, would you be remembered?

One of the many gifts of my illness was that I got to see how many people showed up for my family. My friend Holly and her husband Steve sent me flowers almost every day with cards of love. Holly, my soul sister... we'd grown up from 1st grade together and in all these years, never fought once. We just loved each other. Through all my boyfriends and drama, for her, there was always Steve. But she always listened to me, bad choice after bad choice, and never judged.

My romantic life wasn't typical. For some reason, I attracted drama and men who lived in the spotlight. I gravitated toward them as they did to me. There was the rock star I had loved wholeheartedly. He had started as a friend, and over the years that friendship evolved into a romantic relationship. We would talk for hours by phone as he traveled the world for concerts and I would meet up with him whenever possible. I was that woman on the side of a stage, handing him the towel to wipe his brow as he gazed at me with an intense look and played his guitar. Thousands of fans screamed, cheering on his band to songs they knew by heart, and I would think, I'm living a dream. He was very kind, but he admitted he was incapable of fidelity, and I had to make the heartbreaking decision to let go and move on.

Then there was the world-famous magician whose idea of a romantic date was watching reruns of his television shows. There was a middle eastern Prince who I was convinced, could be my future husband but had to run from when I realized he wouldn't allow me any life choices. Once I was on a weekend trip to London with him when I learned he had decided I was 'the one' and would make a perfect wife for him. He thought a blonde, educated American would make a good wife for a diplomat. When we were at dinner in a chic Berkeley Square restaurant, he'd handed me photographs of a massive mansion in the desert of Abu Dhabi and promptly told me I would be living there. If that wasn't awkward enough, I made the mistake

77

of ordering my meal directly from the waiter, who happened to be male, and the Prince blew up at me… stating that I was not 'allowed' to speak to other men. Later that night, I managed to sneak out of the hotel with the help of a handsome young American living in London. Thank goodness a friend in Boston had misgivings about my cross Atlantic date and had given a heads up to a friend living in the UK who was standing by in case I needed help. The man who helped me escape was a dashing 'hero' himself, and let's just say, he and I had our own 'romantic' weekend. Did I mention I'd flown first class and sat next to a charming British businessman named David? We'd exchanged numbers after he expressed his concern about my weekend plans. We dated off and on for several years too… meeting up in London or Paris for romantic weekends.

My life was a rollercoaster of drama and relationships with high profile and powerful men. I fell in love quickly, and Holly was always there to help pick up the pieces and would just listen to the crazy stories, loving me through it all.

There were several years where I was in a relationship with a public relations guru whose parties were the toast of Boston. We were on and off for years as he was quietly cruel and condescending, but we'd be seen smiling in the social pages of Boston newspapers. He'd shower me with love one minute, then leave me standing at my door, dressed for a black-tie event, rejected because my hairstyle wasn't what he'd have selected, the next. He was one of Boston's most eligible bachelors, and I was caught up in the glamour of the relationship, letting it overshine the more important qualities that were missing. I hadn't learned yet that being treated with kindness and respect consistently was more important than any of the superficial experiences he had to offer.

Life with him was an emotional rollercoaster. For example, one day, he called me at work to ask me to cut the day short and join him for an 'experience' I'd never forget. He wouldn't tell me anything about it but reassured me; I'd enjoy the day and meet someone I'd be excited to meet. Considering he worked with the most prominent musicians in the world, political leaders, and all of Boston sports teams, I was curious and could not resist. He had called me at my place of work at the time, a recruiting firm in Boston. I was drinking in those days and not the most responsible person. I was also easily manipulated by my boyfriend, who could swing from incredibly kind to abusive. When he called me and suggested that I meet him for a 'surprise' short trip that he thought I'd enjoy, I thought, why not?

But I had to find a way to get out of work and not being the most creative of people; I told my boss that my Grandmother was sick. Being of partially Irish descent, I was more than a little superstitious, so I thought the fact that both my Grandmothers had already passed, I wasn't jinxing anyone.

When I left the building I worked in; I found a limousine waiting out front. The window rolled down, and my boyfriend waved me over. Let's call him Greg. It wasn't unusual to travel by limousine, so that didn't surprise me, but we drove for about an hour, and I kept asking him what we were doing but to no avail as he ignored me and took meetings on the phone until we pulled into a small private airport. I asked him if I was dressed appropriately, since I had no idea what we were doing (he often told me how to dress, I should have realized that wasn't a healthy sign) and eyeing me up and down, he gave me approval for the conservative suit I was wearing. All he would tell me is that we had to 'pick up' a famous person.

We rushed through the tiny airport by airline employees who escorted us to a small jet that was waiting on us. It seemed like the most exciting and romantic experience you could imagine, something right out of 'Pretty Woman' only I wasn't a prostitute, and he wasn't Richard Gere. The interior of the plane seemed to light up with the magnificent colors of the setting sun; I reached out to hold his hand only to be brushed aside and ignored as he talked on the phone. As I looked at the sunset, I felt more alone than I had ever felt and wondered what I was even doing there.

My boyfriend was wrapped up in business and could not find the time to tell me where we were going or what we were doing in any detail until we landed. He had opened a bottle of champagne and kept my glass full. Later in the relationship, I'd come to realize that alcohol was a problem for me, and I had told him of my desire to 'cut back.' His response was to continue to ply me with wine, and I came to learn that it was his way of controlling me. He liked keeping me in a state of inebriation as I was more 'manageable' that way.

But back to the jet, after a few hours of drinking the champagne, I looked around the small plane and didn't see a bathroom. I asked Greg where it was, and he pointed to a seat behind the pilot and told me to draw the curtains and pop up the seat. There was no way in hell I was going to relieve myself with so little privacy, so I crossed my legs and prayed I'd make it to Mississippi, the only detail he'd managed to share with me about our plan for the day.

As we neared our destination, he finally told me what we were doing. We were picking up Senator Al Gore, who was running for the Democratic presidential nomination. Greg was responsible for escorting him to the debate at a major news network in Boston. Greg also told me that I shouldn't be there at all, being his girlfriend, since this was a business trip and not giving me an option, he said that I was to pretend that I was a public relations account manager who worked for him.

As the jet approached our destination, all I could think about was finding a bathroom. We landed at a military airbase, and after the plane landed, I ran through the airport in search of a ladies' room. As I ran, I passed several very tall, good-looking men who reached out their hands to introduce themselves, which I promptly ignored as my focus was on the bathroom door behind them.

After joyfully relieving myself, I had freshened up and much calmer, walked back into the airport to realize the tall men I'd ignored were two bodyguards, and Senator Gore himself. They were understanding and gracious, and we all boarded the plane, with a few other men who had joined our small group. After an hour of everyone (except me, who knew better) sipping champagne or wine, one of the bodyguards looked around the plane and asked the same question I had asked earlier. Where was the bathroom? I pointed to the seat, which was now being utilized by a news reporter, and stated, "just ask that reporter to move, pull up the seat and draw the curtains." I guess I wasn't the only one with a shy bladder as that pretty much stopped the drinking, and everyone crossed their legs for the remainder of the flight.

Even though I had the awkward situation of having to pretend I knew what I was talking about when asked about the 'agenda' for the day and the structure of the debate, I did get to spend a few hours in the company of an incredibly impressive Senator Gore. He was kind, intelligent, clearly cared about the future health of our earth, and loved our country. He was a perfect gentleman and spent some time checking in with his wife and family during the flight. We had a fantastic conversation about the state of the environment as he sat right across from me, and we had several hours to kill on our trip to Boston. When we finally landed, everyone on the plane was desperate to find a bathroom, and there was a rush for the exit stairwell. Just as I stepped down in the darkness of the evening, bright light turned on, blinding us, and my boyfriend whispered, we're live on the 11 PM news. My only thought was damn; I can't be seen on the news getting off a plane with a Senator! I told my boss my Grandmother was sick! That was just one example of how crazy a rollercoaster my life was during those years.

Greg was a jet setter, but as I mentioned earlier, he was incredibly controlling and emotionally abusive. One day he kicked me out of his car in the middle of a blizzard because I'd said something he didn't agree with, and I'd had to struggle to find my way home, which was several miles away. I was in high heels, a thin silk wrap, and tripping through snowdrifts had tears freezing on my face. He was also incapable of fidelity, and it took me several years to realize that all the excitement and glamour of the relationship were empty and unsatisfying. Never mind the emotional abuse. I just didn't have the confidence at the time to believe I deserved something better, something healthier.

I'd tried to break up with him countless times, but Greg always managed to convince me how sorry he was and that he'd changed, but of course, he never did. It took me getting sober to learn that I was worthy of being loved and treated with kindness and respect.

If not for close friends, who helped me learn what love looked like, I don't know that I'd be who I am. That I'd have had the courage to walk away from the chase for 'romantic love' and instead have the courage to begin my own family by adopting and becoming a single mother. I learned that I didn't need someone else to take care of me but that I could gain financial stability and take care of myself. I could take care of a child without a life partner. It may not have been what I'd dreamed of, but I'd found joy and fulfillment.

My life became complete by loving another with my whole being, a child who needed me as much as I needed her. I'd found the love I'd sought for years, not through men who were incapable of providing a committed relationship. The love I found was by providing a home for a precious child and focusing not on my needs but hers. Now, I can live my life in peace, truly happy.

I find joy in simple things like being able to pay my bills, provide a comfortable home for my daughter, and spending time with people I love.

I haven't given up on romantic love, I've just turned that over to God. I was trusting that he'll bring someone into our life that's right for us. Someone capable of loving my daughter and me unconditionally. Someone kind, down to earth, who loves animals and has an optimistic outlook on life. Of course, it wouldn't hurt if he was handy around the house, had been in service to our country, had a great sense of humor, and was sexy to boot. In the meanwhile, I had to focus on something much more straightforward than all of that. I needed to survive and gain my physical strength and good health back.

My close friends, Bill and Terry, had started a group text when they learned of my surgery, to support one another they shared stories about me and our friendship over the years. They found laughter and stress relief in reliving some of our mutual life experiences. When I learned about it, I asked if I could join. I wanted to laugh at myself too. Those group texts were now keeping me sane and centered.

People I barely knew from church showed up with offers to help, and one woman I barely knew from work sent me the coziest blanket. The day I got that package, I had found myself facing my image in the mirror. The front half of my head was bald, and I had other bald spots shaved on the top and back of my head. It was scary looking. I still had liquid oozing out of my eyes that freaked me out more than a little. The day the blanket came, there was also a small-cap. Blue and sparkly, nothing my conservative self would have ever picked out, but it was so beautiful and girly. It arrived just as I was beginning to wonder how I would go out and face the world. How had a practical stranger known just what to send? I later learned that her mother had recently passed from breast cancer, so she intuitively knew what to give.

An old friend from Boston, who I had not seen in years, sent me a box full of the most beautiful scarves. I was being taken care of, and I started to let myself accept the love I did not even know was in my life. I had the gift of hearing words that might have been at my funeral, of having friends share with me their wackiest memories, the things they loved about me, and the ways I had touched their lives. These were 'my' people, the ones who would show up when life was at its worst.

I still saw the ghosts. As I struggled to get around the first floor of my house, building up my strength and reconnecting my brain with my limbs, I could zip around sitting on a walker with wheels and a little seat. As I

82

moved around, they were there. When I sat on my couch, I could see them rushing by, whispering, but only after dusk. I strained to hear what they were saying, but a part of me knew I wasn't meant to hear. I am not sure that they were even there for me, and I wasn't afraid of them anymore. I realized they were a part of our world – these spirits – and I didn't necessarily need to communicate with them so much as accept them. I found myself wondering if perhaps they were angels instead of ghosts and felt comforted by that thought, that gentle wings and prayers may surround us from ethereal beings who just want to watch over and protect us as we go about our daily lives.

The world was new to me... the colors brighter, the air softer. I listened to soft piano and cello music, and the notes surrounded me. Was life always this beautiful?

My taste buds and sense of smell continued to reawaken slowly, and I savored fresh fruit, a slice of warm bread... a cup of smooth coffee. Kajal had even picked some grapes growing on our small backyard vine and brought them to me. She didn't care for the gardening that we did. She couldn't fully understand my joy and amazement that we could plant something and grow food (the city girl in me was still in awe of that fact), but she was so focused on finding ways to help me, to make me happy, that she'd picked the early grapes and presented them to me in a tiny bowl. It was the first thing my brain recognized through taste. They were the most delicious food I could ever remember experiencing the velvety texture of the skin, the burst of muscadine juice as I bit into them.

I was so full of gratitude for every second of life that my heart seemed to be bursting with joy, and all I wanted to do, was love back. Love the world, love every person that came across my path.

My fear of work seemed to slip away even as I knew I'd be returning to a different environment, one where I'd been undermined by someone I had trusted entirely. I'd finally come to accept that the woman who turned on me must have her issues, and even though what she did was pretty bad, I knew it wouldn't change the way I treated her. I'd still be supportive and kind; I'd forgive her actions... I just wouldn't forget. Life showed me who she was, and there was no anger wrapped up in reality, just acceptance. It's a gift when you learn who you can trust, who is there for you and who is not.

Faith

I've come to believe that God brings people into our lives for a reason. To push us to grow and become the people we're meant to be. Letting go of resentments and learning to celebrate the lessons we learn, appreciating the good in our lives, the simple and the pure.

I always thought I'd get married to Mr. Right, settle down, and be taken care of in life. Instead, all those broken relationships led to my being a woman who was strong enough to travel to India and become a single mother. To advance in my career not through ambition, but for being my best every day. For showing up and giving life and work my all, from a place of authenticity. Extending kindness and generosity to others came naturally for me, and the greatest gift was all those that supported me now.

It's so easy to get caught up in the wants and must-haves to put pressure on ourselves to be more and have more. I remembered one of the first pictures I saw of Kajal. She was smiling and not just an average, 'hey I'm happy' smile but a radiant smile, a smile that came from her soul. I thought, here is a child who has nothing, no one to love her, no clothes or shoes to call her own… not even the knowledge she'll have food in times of hunger, yet here she is smiling, with a joy so profound it must have come from another place.

I thought if a child can smile with the purest joy when she has nothing, imagine the spirit that she must have? The strength and faith that comes from a soul so deep, not even the worst of life can knock it free.

I remember how I first began to discover God, how my faith was born. It wasn't through the church. My mother was Catholic, my father Jewish. We went to Sunday school with Father Joseph and summer Jewish camp in the Catskill mountains. Can you imagine the confusion?

I had traveled to the Virgin Islands with a few close friends for a spontaneous weekend. My friend Kathy was a travel agent, and she had an invitation to visit and stay in a villa, and she shared that invitation with another friend and me. We flew down on a Thursday, and by Friday, we knew a hurricane was headed straight for us. We were stuck on St. Croix because all the planes had already been evacuated from the island. The storm hit on Saturday late afternoon and lasted through the night. Hurricane Hugo was a Category 5 when it hit the little island with all its force. It created three tornadoes that ripped right through the villa where we were staying. Our lives were saved by lying on a flooded muddy floor while grasping mattresses over our heads. Broken glass, metal, and bugs floated around us. When we finally dug our way out to see the devastated landscape around us, it looked like a nuclear bomb had struck.

We saw crushed cars and homes ripped apart and people walking in ripped clothes with a dazed look upon their faces. Somehow, we'd all survived, even though the villas were torn apart like cardboard houses. People of all races, religions, and backgrounds gravitated to one another, and through shared experience, there existed an immediate mutual love and acceptance. They were helping one another, without question. I thought there must be a God. How else could strangers come together so quickly, without hesitation, to help one another? It was beautiful, and it was right. I joined a group prayer of gratitude, and I started to believe that a power higher than myself had to exist.

Ten days later, the U.S. National Guard and Marines arrived on the island after it was designated a national disaster area and brought actual tanks in to rescue us. When we arrived at the airport it was crushed, you could see the few planes on the ground through the demolished walls of the pre-existing buildings. People were desperate to get on any flight, no matter where it was going… just to get off the island. Hundreds more were asking for help, trying to get messages to loved ones off the island since the mail and phones still weren't working. One woman was waving a letter in the air, asking if anyone was going to Boston. She needed help in delivering an urgent message. There was desperation in her voice.

I asked her how I could help, and she explained that there was a teenager who was severely burned and had given up on life. He wasn't eating, and his grandfather, his only living relative, lived on St. Croix and was scheduled to fly out to see him the week the hurricane had hit. Would I deliver the letter? The boy was at the Shriners Burn Hospital for Children in Boston. It was more than a coincidence; it was another example of God connecting us to people who need us, guiding us with invisible hands. To back up a little, my mother always taught me the importance of giving back from the time I was an incredibly young child. When I turned 14, she drove me to the nearest hospital and signed me up to be a candy striper.

By the time I'd reached college, I was volunteering for an organization that granted wishes for seriously ill children and had granted so many requests that I'd become what they referred to as an 'emergency wish granter.' The organization granted wishes for critically, chronically, or seriously ill children, but on occasion, they were racing against the clock and may only have hours before the child may pass. That is when they called me in, to grant an 'emergency wish' and find a way with very little time, to identify a child's wish and creatively, make it come true. So, here I was, an experienced wish granter, who lived not only in Boston but literally across the street from the Shriners Burn Hospital. I told her I'd deliver the letter in person and let the boy know his Grandfather was alright. I'd then try and find out what was keeping him from eating and see if a wish granted would help him heal somehow – perhaps just by giving him hope that something good could happen to him.

When I arrived back in Boston, I visited with the teen, Peppi. He was burned over 90% of his body and had given up on life and given up hope. We spent hours together talking, and somehow, I was able to reach him. His horrific story involved losing his two best friends in the same fire he'd survived in a children's home on the island. His only wish was to feel like a real teenager again; without the stares, he knew he would receive with his burned face and body. So that was his wish, and I was determined to grant it. He started to eat again, and I visited him several times a week. When he was well enough to spend a few hours away from the hospital, a nurse brought him to the Hard Rock Café where the staff and diners had been prepared in advance what to expect. He ate a hamburger and enjoyed some rude teasing from the waiters; he received a whole new wardrobe and some of his favorite music. He was a typical teenager for a day. His hope returned fully, and he started to fight to live again.

I was on that island, survived that hurricane only to deliver a life-saving message to a teenager who was lost and alone. If that's not God working, I don't know what is.

Perhaps this tumor was just another one of life's experiences to set me up for something better than I could have imagined for myself.

After Hurricane Hugo, the seed of faith was planted, but I came home to a significant loss that sent me in a downward spiral leading to what became years of alcohol abuse. I was still in love with Jason (my mobster boyfriend). I'd 'forgiven' him his multitude of charges of racketeering he was 'serving' time after all. The romantic in me saw past all the rumors and the actual criminal charges, and we had been writing letters while he was in prison ... I know, talk about being desperate for love and separated from any sense of decent reality. He had known of my trip and had been in a panic trying to reach me. When he learned I had survived the storm (literally), he wrote of his undying love and asked to see me upon his release from prison.

My life with Jason had been surreal. I met him while I was in college at a nightclub he owned in Boston. I was in my early twenties; he was a dashing late twenty-something with a sense of humor combined with a shyness that quickly captured my heart. I heard rumors that he was from a powerful Italian family, but I disregarded them as I genuinely didn't believe such things existed. We'd become friends first, and he quickly became very protective of me. At the time, a close college friend and I had become the toasts of Boston. We were young and blonde and attracted attention everywhere we went. Doors opened to a prominent social crowd, and we were often in the company of celebrities, rock stars, politicians, sports stars, etc. It was a whirlwind life, and Jason was at the center of it for me.

Before I knew it, I had limousines taking me on errands and Jason's very large and muscular, 'best buddies' watching out for me everywhere I went. We drove around town in his Ferrari and dined in the best restaurants, treated as local celebrities. It was easy to get caught up in the glamour and attention, to be swept away, ignoring all the warning signs, i.e., gun-toting 'friends' that watched our every move. I was a nut, a champagne drinking space-cadet.

When Jason was released, we spent a romantic weekend together. Dining in a tiny romantic Italian restaurant, he told me he wanted to marry me and spend our lives together. I never stopped to think about how we'd managed this. Would we be sheltered away on his island compound, avoiding competing 'families' and the FBI? But that's all it took to win me over, and a few months later, I found out I was pregnant. Instead of being overwhelmed with fear, I felt it was a sign we were meant to be together, and I began to dream of a life with Jason and our precious child. I reached out to share the good news, but he seemed to have dropped off the earth. He stopped returning my calls; his family and friends wouldn't tell me where he was.

I was heartbroken but determined to bring our child into the world. My friends and family thought I was nuts; if his family were as dangerous as the press had reported, I'd always be looking over my shoulder and hiding from the more dangerous side of his life. It didn't matter to me. I lived in the rosy glow of my pregnancy and denial of the total rejection I'd experienced and shopped for maternity and baby clothes.

When I was just over five months pregnant, I went in for a checkup, and the doctor examining me became intensely concerned. As I waited to hear my little boy's heartbeat (he was a boy!), the doctor looked at me with sadness and told me that my baby hadn't survived. I couldn't process the news. My own heart seemed to stop, and I couldn't breathe. I fought back, arguing with the doctor, and demanding a second opinion. He wanted to perform a DNC to 'clear' out my uterus, but I refused. I felt like he was trying to kill my child, the child I'd begun to love from the moment that stick turned blue. A second doctor came in and confirmed my worst nightmare. I left the office with tears streaming down my face alone.

That was the first time in my life, where all hope was gone and feeling alone... I just didn't want to live. I sat in my apartment, crying as if someone had ripped out my soul, and at some point... days later, I found the energy to do one thing. Drink.

Redemption

When I was younger, in my teens and college years, I'd not been a heavy drinker, but the 'gene' was in me. I'd had an Irish grandmother who loved her beer and whiskey, but I'd never imagined the illness lived in me. I didn't drink daily, but as I got older, I began to drink heavier, to forget, and to dull the pain of some of the heartbreaks I'd experienced in my life. I'd just wanted to grow up and have the white picket fence dreams, but God had other plans for me. It took a lot of broken relationships and personal frustration from clinging to people who weren't healthy for me before I could see through the cloud of alcohol that I used to dull the pain and disappointment. My abuse of alcohol continued for years as I seemed to lose touch with who I was and who I was meant to be.

I worked, I lived, but my faith and soul seemed to be slipping away. Men came and went, and I'd become lonelier and lonelier, making more and more bad choices along the way.

How many times did I get into a car with a stranger, walk across a street without looking? How I'd survived those years is beyond my comprehension. My near-death experiences didn't start with a mobster boyfriend or with alcohol abuse. My life was a series of 'close calls.'

When I was just a year old, I kept getting sick, and my mother believed something was wrong, so she took me to doctors who assured her I was okay, and nothing was wrong. They told her it was likely stress and that she should see a psychiatrist. In those days, women's opinions weren't taken as seriously by men who had been in the medical practice for ages. She didn't give up though and seeing doctors until one found a congenital heart defect that confirmed my mother's worst fears, that my life would be short-lived.

My mother believed I'd overcome the odds and live a full life, and she raised me to think that I was capable of anything.

When I was around ten years old, I remember being in a hospital hallway after some tests and hearing nurses and doctors discussing the fact that I'd likely die young, and I put my hand in my mother's and left the hospital that day and didn't tell a soul what I'd learned. As a child knowing that you are supposed to die at any time, I was not full of fear so much as wondering why; why me? Being raised in a Catholic church, I came to believe that if I were good and didn't 'sin,' I would be saved; so I took this literally and started to pray to God, asking him to 'save' me and promising to be a good, no, a really, really good girl. I did my chores, listened to my parents, never cheated in school, or broke any (well, many) rules, but the prognosis did not seem to change. Years later, I had a cardiac event while walking my dog one morning in Boston. I met with a cardiac specialist who took the time to more appropriately diagnose my heart defect that caused an electrical irregularity that caused heart arrhythmias and a simple medication that would cure me.

When I was a teenager, my family and I were vacationing on Cape Cod, and I met the cutest set of 16-year-old twins (boys) who flattered me with attention and an invitation to go sailing with them on a small sailboat. My mother told me not to go, but the 'good girl' broke free for a few minutes and caved at the invitation. While we were sailing, the boom broke loose as I was gazing at the ocean, and before I could duck, hit me full force on the front of my head and knocked me into the sea. The boys dove in to try and find me but had no success and screamed for help. My parents and people on the beach came rushing but could not see me anywhere. I have a distant memory of falling asleep as my body turned and turned under the ocean waves, peacefully not fighting the current.

A woman walking the beach saw what she thought was a dolphin pushing something covered in seaweed to the shore. She went to investigate and found me unconscious, lying on the beach, and she called 911. I awoke in the hospital, the doctors found no water in my lungs, or permanent damage and I got to face two very angry parents. I wondered how I'd been brought back to the living for no apparent reason. Not to mention I have been grateful to dolphins ever since...

With my long-term health still in question, even as a youngster, I prayed for answers, wondering why I was granted these years of life when time and time again, it seemed I wasn't meant to be. My experience as a sick child is what drew me to grant wishes for other children who may not be so blessed; I felt a kinship with them that went more profound than any adult could understand. My mother always told me I'd survive, and I clung to those words year after year, believing that if I thought I could, I would.

Believing in God is one thing, but understanding that God will be there to watch over you, guide you, and even save you is a bit harder to conceptualize when you've done nothing but screw up your life. People in a church may say that God loves you, but as an active alcoholic who lived a pretty wild lifestyle, it was almost impossible to conceive that God would be interested in helping me out when I'd done little in recent years to deserve His love. I did not feel loveable.

When I was early in my sobriety, I was struggling to become a filmmaker. My colleagues (of the small film company we had started) had been to Sundance, and we were on our way to the Nantucket Film Festival. I was just hitting the 60-day sober mark, and the more stressed I became, the more I was tempted to drink. It was strange because I had never been a daily drinker. I was more of a weekend partier, but when I got sober, all I could think about was how much I wanted to drink. The thought of attending a ten-day film festival with parties every day and evening and liquor flowing non-stop was intimidating. It did not help that when I checked in at the festival, all I saw were signs advertising the vodka company that was sponsoring the event. Talk about torture! The gift bag even had shot glasses in it, and promotional items care of the liquor company. My sponsor in the program had given me a list of meetings on the island and told me to hit one the day I arrived to make sure I had support, but seriously, I knew no one there. How on earth would I get through one day without drinking, never mind 10?

I went to a meeting, though, and raised my hand as I'd been taught and asked for help. Following the meeting, several people approached me and told me they knew my sponsor, and she'd told them of my impending arrival. This community of strangers was offering to help me even though they'd never met me before. Over the coming days, several things happened that were almost indescribable and made little sense in the perfectness of how they unfolded. At one evening party, I had ordered a fruit juice and seltzer drink from the bartender and turned my back to talk with someone from the press. As I went to reach for my glass, a hand stopped me, and I looked up to see a handsome gentleman shaking his head. He heard my story at the meeting and had decided to go to the party because and he wanted to make sure I was okay. When he walked into the restaurant, he saw the bartender pouring vodka into the drink before handing it to me. I was shocked but grateful he had intercepted the apparent error that could have sent me over the edge.

In another instance, I stepped out of a sold-out performance of our film because I had seen an actress I'd always admired, and the pressure of the celebrity presence was overwhelming. Standing outside, I saw a sign advertising the sponsor's vodka, and I started fantasizing about having a martini. I had never been a martini drinker, but suddenly I became obsessed with finding one. As I turned toward the nearest bar, a hand stopped me, and I turned to see a stranger smiling down at me. He reached out and shook my hand, congratulating me on the film's success, and I felt him press something into my palm. I looked down to see what was there and a coin reflected in the sunlight. The man whispered, "I heard that you just celebrated 60 days but didn't have your chip yet." I took a deep breath, and a sense of serenity waved over me. I thanked him for saving me from myself.

Coincidently, before I left for the festival, I had started reading the 2nd step with my sobriety program sponsor, "Came to believe that a power greater than myself could restore me to sanity." I had not believed that God would care one way or another about what happened to me, never mind be willing to help such a spiritual wasteland as I'd felt I'd become. But over those ten days, I slowly came to believe that perhaps God was watching out for me and that I was indeed someone He cared about. That perhaps, I was worth saving after all.

Seeking Answers

For years since I explored different churches, seeking answers. Once I moved down south, finding a church was more of a challenge. Not because there wasn't every kind of church you could imagine on every street corner, but in the south, the churches seemed to be self-segregated, and as a bi-racial family, we didn't seem to 'fit' in anywhere.

After a year or so, we ended up at Seacoast, a non-denominational church whose message of service and acceptance resonated with me, and we settled into its community as well as a working sober, single mom could manage, which was barely at all. I think that is why I was so surprised that a pastor and other members of the congregation showed up for me when I learned about my brain tumor. I honestly did not feel as if I deserved that outpouring of love. Do any of us? Do you?

When someone shows up and loves you… offers to be there for you unconditionally, do you welcome them with open arms thinking, this is just what I deserve? Or do you question their motivations and your worthiness?

Accepting love is hard, but boy, when you learn to, without struggle, it feels like a vacation every day.

So here I am, back among the living, and I find myself struggling with why? It seems like every other person I run into knows someone else who had or has a brain tumor, and every single story, every single one, ends with they weren't as lucky as you. They have either died or are in the process of dying.

So why am I here? I still couldn't get my head around the fact that I'd been living my life, walking around with a killer bomb in my head, and was completely unaware. Many of us wonder, at different times of our lives, why are we here? Are we fulfilling our destiny? Is there such a thing as destiny? We may feel there is a purpose just lurking beyond us that we have not quite discovered yet, but we know exists, a reason for all we experience in life. As we find out what our gifts are, the uniqueness that belongs only to us, shouldn't we find a way to give back? To leverage that uniqueness into our own individual purpose … to create a living legacy, not just through our children but the impact we have on those whose lives we intersect within our daily living.

During my recovery, I could not sit still. I knew that's what I needed to do to heal, but it was almost impossible. I was so used to going non-stop from morning to night that staying in one place for more than a few minutes was a challenge. I didn't have much choice, though, and had to take it easy. I lacked coordination and was weak, and I was drawn more and more to my backyard garden. Calling it a garden is a stretch, as I'd always dreamed of days when I'd have time to create a colorful and wild landscape, but I never found the time. Not to mention that I managed to kill houseplants that were supposed to be able to withstand even the most considerable amount of neglect. I'd planted more by experiment, always in wonder when something survived, never mind flourished.

One of my team members at work led an organization that he and his daughter started called Katies Krops. They supported children who grew gardens to feed the hungry. John had been one of the first people from work to reach out to me when I came home. He had brought nourishment in the form of pasta, homemade Italian gravy, and raspberry lemonade. I fell in love with the lemonade and savored it as if it were the most precious concoction in the world. He shared stories of his own brother's ability to survive and overcome a brain tumor. He talked about his daughter's organization, and the joy his family had in knowing their work resulted in

98

feeding those who were hungry. I was desperate to become 'of value' with this second chance I had been given, and before you knew it, he was helping Kajal build a large raised garden bed in the back yard.

We planted sweet potatoes and carrots, tomatoes, and peppers. I became obsessed with creating a garden to help a food pantry I'd found at a nearby church that helped people in our community who were struggling to make ends meet. Selfishly, I also hoped that creating a garden paradise in our back yard might make it easier for me to stop and find stillness during the day, healing silence. A place to talk with God and perhaps, find some answers. But instead of sitting still and meditating or praying, I just kept building garden beds and planting seeds. Our first harvest was a handful of skimpy, very tiny carrots, but as I delivered them to the pantry, the women worked there didn't judge us or turn us away. They laughed with us and suggested they were the perfect size for dipping. They were half the size of the tiny carrots you find bagged in the grocery store, but it felt good to give something back... even if they didn't fill a small zip lock bag.

Work-Life Balance

As my body relearned to connect with my brain, I started to function on a more normal level, living my life. I was physically doing a million times better. I began to work again, find success in my professional life, and I embraced Kajal with a more profound love for all we had lived through together. I was recovering more each day. As my physical self-found, it's way back to daily functioning; my emotions started to go haywire. My sensitivities were on overdrive, and I found myself bawling at red lights… crying so hard at times, I'd have to pull over or just sit in my driveway trying to work up the emotional strength to walk in the front door. It was crazy.

I went back to work barely two months after surgery. I had miraculously managed to be productive right up until my emergency prognosis, but the people I worked with were treating me with kid gloves, almost to the point of ignoring me. The woman who reported to me and had helped lead my team during my absence, acted as if she was still in charge, and when she communicated with me, it was often with disdain and bold insubordination. With my newly gained, near-death outlook on life, I tried to laugh it off; after all, it wasn't what was important anymore, right? Life was, and my family was. Work was just a means to an end, a way to support those that I love.

I tried not to let my colleague's behavior affect my center of gravity, my peaceful existence, and celebration of being alive. Who cared if the people I used to admire and work closely with, day in and day out, treated me like a pariah… like a woman who had a deadly tumor living in her skull for who knows how many years. The sales team had stopped sending new leads to me and made the excuse they were giving me time to bounce back.

That was a tiny bit frightening. After all, that would only make it harder for me to 'bounce back.' Our leadership often measured our value by the size of our portfolio, and if the sales team were sending all their leads to my colleagues, then I would start to fall further behind, which would justify the belief that I wasn't 'as good' anymore. I had a nagging feeling I was being set up for failure. They were further trying to prove that I was not 'as good' as they initially perceived me to be. I tried not to be resentful that no one seemed to celebrate or acknowledge that I had managed to be incredibly successful, flying around the world and winning multimillion-dollar global clients while barely hanging on to life. It was business as usual, but I knew it wasn't. They expected me to deliver more, and prove that I was in my boss's words '100%'' again. They were setting unrealistic goals, and the damages to my reputation, which had been successfully manipulated by the member of my team whose desire to get ahead, played havoc on my recovery. Her resentment at my return created stress in every conversation, conference call, and meeting that she attended. She was condescending and ignored my directions, and there was nothing I could do because she'd developed such a tight relationship with my boss during my absence. I kept trying to tell myself; this doesn't matter in the big scheme of things. I know what's important now, but financial insecurity still crept in. On top of the challenges I faced at work, leaders of the company were making comments about my 'new' hairstyle. Seriously?

The bangs that I had been growing out to cover my ear to ear scar didn't align with the executive style that was expected of me, and in my leader's mind, a cane was a sign of weakness. So, I had to stash it when I went to meetings where colleagues were in attendance, which increased my level of exhaustion during the day. When I traveled, I had become paranoid about being seen by someone at work because I needed to use wheelchair services to get through the large airports my corporate travel brought me to. I'd find myself tipping the airport workers to hide me behind columns if I saw a colleague in the distance. I always kept my eyes peeled for colleagues in airports when attending out of town meetings and mapped ways to get through the airports to avoid the possibility of 'wheeling' into them.

I was trying to be the same person I was before, but my life was new, and I had to realize, different. There were days when I wanted to rip off my headband, pull back my growing bangs, and show my scar to the world. To expose it outside in the sunshine and scream, this is me! I've survived, and I'm proud of it! I put all my physical strength into work, but I was drained of energy so quickly, constantly being reminded by my body and brain that I was a long way from being 'better.' The term 'work-life balance' had a whole new definition for me in the post brain tumor life I was trying to live. It's incredible how you can live through this massive, earth-shattering experience, and the whole world just keeps going on as if nothing ever happened. People argue over parking spaces, giving each other dirty looks when they get a little too close for comfort on the subway or in the grocery store line. In the Covid-19 world, people stress out over who wears a mask and who doesn't. Who doesn't social distance, and who touched the tomato before they did in the grocery store? Times have changed, and things are more stressful. We're dealing with an illness that puts everyone at risk. Some are taking it seriously, and others can keep moving on with their lives more quickly.

Those of us who may have experienced the loss of a relationship, death of a loved one, a severe diagnosis, or as in my case, literal brain surgery may want to scream at everyone, hello!!! The earth just turned upside down; why are you acting as if everything is so normal!

That is how people coming back from a war zone must feel, or after losing their home to fires or tornadoes. Or yes, even after receiving a life-threatening prognosis. Life and work just keep going, and there you are, standing in the ever-revolving world while you are just moving in slow motion as the shock of life settles in.

I continued to be productive because that is what you have to do. Wake up, brush your teeth, go to work, and do whatever it is you do. But you find yourself wondering, why? I was trying to understand why I'd been saved and what God wanted from me. Was this what it was all about, only this? Doing everything I could to prove myself, hanging on to a job where I was miserable and treated with disrespect?

My assistant helped me through each day, reminding me of appointments that my short-term memory would have missed. Still, my ability to focus on the computer or conference calls became more difficult as the pain in my head continued to increase. As the stress at work continued, the pain increased and became unbearable. There just had to be more to life than constantly worrying about whether I was 'good enough' and to hanging on to a job that was becoming more and more physically challenging to maintain.

I was terrified of losing my position and not being able to provide for my family. What did God want me to do?! He must have wanted something, or I would not be here, right? Was it to return to a position where I had to continually look over my shoulder to keep an eye on the corporate sharks? To spend time worrying about my nails being the perfect color or that my Hermes scarf completed my outfit just so, my hairstyle was acceptable – or was there something more? There had to be something more...

I did not know what was in store for me, but as I tried to have faith, a depression had crept in as I battled my pain and the memories of the recent weeks I'd survived. It was hard to move forward when I still felt shaken to the soul at what I'd lived through and the question of why, why it happened, why I was alive, what was it all about permeated my every day. The trauma of the experience seemed to become a part of my daily living.

Newfie Therapy

I had no clue what was really in store for me as I became more open to a higher purpose for my life, the desire to begin to give back, and hopefully have some level of positive impact on the world around me. I'd made a promise to God when I was in the emergency room, that if I survived, I would have a therapy dog as well and pass on the hope and momentary escape from reality that Raider had given to me. I have come to believe that all we can do is the next right thing. I had searched desperately for meaning, for something more important than making my company another million in profits. I knew I needed to contribute to the world in a more personal way, and Raider had given me the answer of where to start. Don't get me wrong, being a mother to Kajal has been and probably will forever be, the most significant purpose of my life, but she was growing up and didn't need me as much anymore. There are future foster/adopt children in my life, but that is the future. I needed to fulfill my desperate, near end of life promise, to make a difference now.

Kajal and I started to investigate different dog breeds. I've always loved Cavaliers, but after losing Logan and Bear, two Cavaliers in a relatively short period, I felt the one we had, Amber, was enough. I decided it was time for a big dog, a huge dog. To go the opposite direction from the toy breeds I'd embraced for so long. That and I'd had a Great Dane when I was growing up, and her antics have led to many outrageous stories that I'd shared with Kajal, and I wanted her to have similar experiences. So, we researched the different giant breeds. St. Bernard's, Bernese Mountain, and Leonberger's... my friend, Joanne, reminded me how much I'd loved her Newfoundland's, Woody, and Plato. It had been a long time, but as she shared stories of their naughtiness and kindness, I grew more and more convinced. Kajal and I would sit up late into the evening, researching them on the computer. Once we realized they were known for being great therapy dogs as well as the most natural water rescue dogs in the world, we became hooked. Living in a state with water everywhere you looked, it seemed incredibly appropriate.

We explored rescue but couldn't find any available Newfoundland's in our area, so we started to research breeders. We stumbled across TimberKnoll Newfoundland's, a breeder in North Carolina who had started their kennel almost 20 years earlier after they rescued 10 Newfies from a backyard breeder. With that kind of heart, how could they not be a perfect fit for us? They raised their dogs in their home and didn't over breed or give up on them once they'd retired and grown old. Their dogs were part of their family, and we knew they were who we wanted to get our new fur baby from. We called and wrote but to no avail. They ignored our correspondence. I'd filled out an online application, and finally, I decided to write a letter. Kajal sat with me as I started to type. 'Put it all out there, Mom, do whatever it takes,' and so I did. Before I knew it, the story of my surgery poured out, and our commitment to the breed and therapy work.

I guess that spoke to their hearts because I got a call that day, and we talked for almost an hour. We connected on so many levels, and before we knew it, we were expecting! How do you prepare for a massive furball to enter your lives? We read through all the literature online, bought the breed books, and the giant stainless-steel water bowl. We got the crate that filled up half of our kitchen, the giant breed puppy food, chew toys, and grooming tools. We researched the best safety harnesses for the long trek to TimberKnoll's mountain home and begged our neighbor Patty to drive us. I was not driving much yet, and being from Boston had never driven on a highway. Did I mention I only got my license right before we moved to South Carolina, and my driving experience was limited to the burbs? It was only a few months post-surgery, and I was still struggling with some daily pain and thought processes, so I did not trust myself to handle such a long drive.

The drive up the mountain was terrifying. We were suburbanites, and the trip was hazardous. The sign should have warned us at the entrance to the mountain that announced, '4-wheel drive's only'. We looked at each other, and Patty asked me, do you have a 4-wheel drive? It was the new Lexus I had gotten myself as a Christmas present (actually made the salesman drive it out of the dealership with the giant red bow on it). It was my post-surgery, major gift to myself thinking that you have to live once, right? Of course, it didn't occur to me that my post tumor brain wasn't exactly capable of controlling impulse purchases. Does all-wheel drive count? Thinking it was the same thing, but not knowing as you were talking to three people that wouldn't know where the engine was. We assumed we'd be okay, and we headed up the mountain.

It was just beginning to snow, and let's just say; there were no guard rails on this road. The mountainside, although beautiful, was treacherous, and the side of the road was a cliff that descended thousands of feet. Curve after blind curve, we drove as the clouds thickened, and the snow started to fall. We were praying, and at one point, we were all in tears of fear. This was nuts! But we were determined to get our arms around that perfect ball of black fluff. After driving to the top of the mountain without any idea where we were, we managed to pull off at an actual fork in the road. God, was this a message or what? Standing on the street, trying to get a phone signal to call Benita (owner of the kennel) when a pickup truck pulled over, and an old lady with waist-length hair pulled up. We weren't sure if she'd be pulling out a shotgun, and as we held our breath, she flipped her waist-length grey hair over her shoulder and kindly offered to help us. We told her we were looking for a house that had a group of massive dogs, and she immediately knew the house we were talking about. She guided us safely to the entrance of TimberKnoll. Benita had to come up and drive the car up the driveway because even that looked like a 90 degree straight up, drive from hell.

At this point, we were emotionally exhausted, and after we said our hello's, I just wanted to nab our puppy and be on our way. Benita had other plans, though, and drilled me with questions about our plans for the puppy.

107

Even though we'd already been through what seemed like a thousand questions before getting to this point, she and her partner Patti were serious about who they sold their champion bred puppies to. She wasted no time letting me know that she'd turned away buyers before if she had any doubt that they could be trusted, responsible, loving, and safe homes for their cherished and sought-after puppies. The contract was longer than the real estate agreement to purchase my house, and my recently recovered brain had trouble processing the information. We had to commit to feeding certain types/brands of dog food, grooming with a specific type of brush, showing, and training, it went on and on, but there was no stopping me at this point. We were not leaving without a TimberKnoll puppy. I was on a personal mission guided by the big man upstairs, and there was no doubt this was meant to be. We passed the inspection (barely after Benita realized I didn't have a crate in the car for safe travel, and I had to show her the special puppy harness/seat belt we'd researched up the ying-yang). She led us to a porch and readied us for the Newfie introductions.

A door opened, and a mass of giant bears rushed out and surrounded us. Kajal and I ended up on the ground being licked and smelled and pawed at by the most gentle and furry creatures we'd ever come across. They were the big dogs, the mother Sunee, and her siblings and cousins. Each one was bigger than the last. Then it was time to meet our puppy. Benita and Patti opened a gate, and a half a dozen rolly polly bear cubs came flying out. They were running in every direction, but one ran straight for me. The ball of shiny black fur had a red ribbon around his neck, and he landed in my lap and curled up as if he'd just found where he belonged. And he had. "Well, can you believe that?" Benita said, and sure enough, the 27 pounds, 10-week old bear cub was TimberKnoll's Water Warrior Chewbacca, 'Chewie.'

Remember how I mentioned that God has a way of creating good from bad in our lives? Benita and Patti were two of the top breeders in the country, but they'd taken a chance on us, even though they'd had a waiting list. I learned later how unusual that was for them that most of their puppies went to families they knew well or were well known in 'Newfie' circles. They were touched when they had realized we were following a faith-based path to make a difference, and they wanted to support that. That day, we gained more than a puppy, Benita, and Patti became our close friends and, in time, more than close friends... they became part of our family.

Puppies are puppies, though, even those from championship homes. There was not a computer or phone cord that was safe. Chewie was teething and chewing through anything he could find. Keep in mind; this was not your average puppy either. He was over 30 pounds within 48 hours and was growing as fast as we fed him. He was a mass of black flying fur and even more massive paws that managed to squirm his way past or over every puppy gate we installed. There wasn't a shoe, a lamp, even a wall that was safe. We bought every toy we could find to entertain him, signed him up for BarkBox (a monthly service that delivers toys and treats to your door) and kept a huge box of dog cookies on the counter ready to distract him whenever he was chewing on something that could cause him, or us, danger. We were terrified he'd get shocked, cause a fire, or even chewed his way through a wall to get out of a room we'd corned him in. We tried to crate train him, but he'd cry, and my heart just couldn't take it. I'd sleep on the ground next to his crate, my hand stroking his paw through the grates, but he'd cry until I'd cave and let him out.

We must have called Benita and Patti every day, for advice about absolutely everything he did, and they continued to guide us on this new journey of Newfie care and understanding. Their patience was unending, and they never judged us, no matter how ridiculous or straightforward our questions would be. They laughed with us over his antics, encouraged us, and offered advice on training tips to get us started on obedience, therapy, and water rescue techniques.

It was like having a wild animal in the house, but the cutest, most affectionate, loving, and gentle, wild animal you'd ever know. We began to teach him the basic obedience commands, and one day he'd 'get' them, and we bragged about how brilliant he was. The next, he would act like we were speaking a foreign language that he'd never heard before. He grew so fast he was surfing the counters in no time, and nothing was safe. His paws were massive, like bear claws, and we could not help but wonder how large he'd grow. One day we came home and found him standing up, like a person, with one furry black paw wrapped around the box of dog cookies and the other paw reaching into the box, scooping out cookies and popping them in his mouth. He had gone through half the box by the time we'd stopped laughing, snapped out of our shock, and been able to reach him.

We went to our neighborhood Petco and signed him up for a full round of training classes, from puppy through adulthood. We didn't want to take any chances that he'd grow so big we couldn't handle him. We focused on training him through every level of obedience class, but he didn't make it easy. Their training was based on positive reinforcement only, and treats were a big part of that training. Chewie was picky about dog cookies and wouldn't hesitate to spit one out if it didn't meet his standards, which were known only to him and changed for every class we'd attend.

Before we knew it, Chewie was graduating with his Canine Good Citizen award and was so huge he towered over his trainer in graduation photos, and the cap they balanced on his head was about three sizes too small. He may have behaved well when he was out in the world being adored by his growing fan base in our town, but at home, he'd become incredibly naughty. His counter surfing had advanced, and there was nothing he wouldn't grab and smash or eat.

If he asked to go outside, either by talking with his goofy deep voice or barking for attention, and we didn't snap to his attention, he'd walk over to a table and right in front of us, grab something he knew he shouldn't have. It could be a tv remote, pen, or a full glass of water, and right in front of us, he'd shake it as if to say, 'now will you let me out?'. Chewie had seen us snacking on the couch watching television and learned from us. It wasn't unusual for him to grab a loaf of bread or even a bag of oranges he'd take it from the counter and confidently walk over and climb on the couch next to us, totally shameless. It was his couch, too, after all. He grew, and before we knew it, our puppy was beginning to look more like a huge black bear than a dog. As we prepared for our therapy certification, I noticed some more unusual behaviors that were more intuitive and would leave me speechless.

You must remember, through all this, my head was in pain all the time. Between juggling and managing the stress of home, single motherhood, taking care of my mother, and this crazy, wild, gigantic new dog... I was exhausted. One day when I was sitting at my desk, my head throbbing as I tried to focus on the computer. Chewie was seated near me, and he came over to me and leaned his huge head against mine. His forehead rested against my own, and he nuzzled my face ever so gently. I wrapped my arms around him and leaned into him until the pain passed. He seemed to know what I needed, better than I knew myself. When I experienced weakness, he would push into me as if to guide me to the nearest chair. He would awaken

110

me when nightmares of my diagnosis ravaged my sleep, his head resting on the bedside nudging me awake and then licking my face until my breathing slowed, and I could rest peacefully again. He would walk beside me as I climbed the stairs or grew tired walking through the house. He howled if we were separated, and his gaze followed me as if waiting for me to need him in one of his peculiar ways. Who would have known that this dog we'd gotten for serving others, would end up helping me in ways well beyond anything I could have dreamed or imagined?

Learning to Lean

Emotionally, I was suffering from post-traumatic stress from the shock of processing how close I'd come to calling it a day. I was a rollercoaster of emotions and tears that seemed to come out of nowhere. Then there was the pain. It was different from the first month's post-surgery pain. The nerves the doctors said would never come back to life in my head had plans of their own. The numbness in my scalp became like lightning bolts, and before I knew it, I had an electronic light show taking place inside my head. I knew it was miraculous that I was alive and functioning, walking, and talking. But then the nerves that had been cut through in surgery and shocked into submission by the presence of my massive head invader came back to life; it was with electric, hot, knife-slicing fury. I never knew when they would hit, but one thing I knew, any tiny bit of stress or emotion would set them raging. At times, it felt like someone had a knife they were scraping across my skull. The doctor told me it was neuropathy, and he wasn't sure how long it would last. It could be a few months, or it could be permanent, only time would tell.

The electric pain was different than the crushing pain, sometimes they came together, and other times one would follow the other. There seemed to be pressure like a vice that was pressing my head with force, unlike anything I remembered experiencing. It came at me from the top and the sides and would last for hours on end. Chewie sensed when the pain was coming and would come to me and lean his massive body against me, offering comfort and support from falling due to the weakness the pain seemed to cause. The pain became my constant companion as it would come in waves throughout my day. On some days, it woke me up and lasted throughout the day until I finally crashed in exhaustion at night. I found that I needed to take two short naps during the day and work a more extended day to make up for it. It wasn't sleeping so much that I needed, but to close my eyes and cut out the electric light of the computer and the simple sights and sounds of the world around me. Chewie would lie snoring at my feet if I snoozed on the couch, and Kajal would tiptoe around the house after she came home from school.

I accepted the pain as part of my life; it seemed it was the price for survival, and I was determined not to let it get me down. I didn't want to lose this precious new joyous appreciation for life and this more profound connection to God that grew out of those long weeks of sitting awake following my surgery. I missed the magical presence that seemed to surround me in those weeks when I knew that God was in the room with me, keeping me alive and comforted in His peaceful light, but he'd also brought me Chewie, who became my new constant companion. He just seemed to 'get' it. When the pain grew louder, he would silently appear, pressing his wet nose against my forehead, licking away the pain as my breath slowed and my arms wrapped around him. When I struggled up the stairs, he would guide me and lead the way, one slow step at a time so that I could lean on him or pull my way up hanging on to his fur.

He'd continue to awaken me in the middle of the night when the recurring nightmares left me sweaty and blinded with pain, and he'd let me lean on him as we walked outside. This dog I'd gotten to be more than a family pet, to be of service and give back to others as I'd been given to, was becoming my own personal miracle. He was being of service to 'me.'

I researched what a service dog was under the Americans with Disabilities Act and learned that he met all the qualifications because of the tasks that he performed to help me. I registered him as a Service Dog, and he started to accompany me almost everywhere. You can just imagine the reaction we had from people as we walked into a store or restaurant. This massive hairy dog would sometimes intimidate or even terrify those that met him, just by his huge and majestic presence, but mostly, people fell instantly in love and would ask to take his picture and pose with him. He was the big shaggy dog from their childhood dreams and brought joy to all those he met. I knew that service dogs weren't supposed to be patted, but since Chewie had also been trained as a therapy dog, I felt it was important that he share his love with others whenever possible. I shouldn't have been surprised at all that Chewie could naturally do; the more I learned about his heritage, the more I realized he'd come from a long line of therapy and water rescue dogs. This was his legacy.

One thing that people who are attracted to Newfs need to accept is that they are droolers, and Chewie is no exception. Newfoundland dogs drool because they need to, it's part of their anatomy. Their large jowls help them as they grab people in the ocean and pull them to rescue. The jowls allow water and air to flow through their mouth as they swim, pulling people to safety. They've been saving people from drowning for hundreds of years. Their webbed feet and legs swim a powerful breaststroke rather than the dog paddle; this enables them to be the most powerful swimmers of all dog breeds and makes them the incredible rescue dogs they are. They even have built-inn eye goggles, film over their eyes that allow them to see underwater so that they can do dive and rescue. But back to the drool. Chewie is no exception. He's a drooler. It's incredible. Sometimes he'll share it by shaking his head and sending it as far as a distant wall, ceiling, or whoever or whatever stands in its way. We see it coming, and we'll duck as it flies towards us. We love the sound of his jowls slapping against his face as he shakes his head from side to side. If you're lucky enough to get a kiss from this mighty animal, you'll have a swipe of an enormous tongue from chin to the tip of your forehead, and you'll come away with saliva dripping down your face. You'd be amazed how many people just laugh in joy as they wipe it away while others might cringe and run for cover.

Kajal and I worked with trainers to prepare him for therapy work, and then Kajal would work with him on water rescue training activities. We began to develop deeper relationships with Benita and Patti at TimberKnoll by traveling to visit them for training days, deep in the heart of their new

115

Smoky Mountain home. This magnificent and gentle soul brought us the gift of friends who were meant to be in our life. They accepted us unconditionally as they taught us all about our new furry family member. Their home was so peaceful; it seemed easier to find silence and stillness. The morning was a warm cup of coffee with prayer and meditation sitting on their porch overlooking the lake and mountains. It was the serene setting I needed to reduce the pain and start facing my experience.

I was still haunted by the question of what my higher purpose in life was. Being a good mother, daughter, sister, and friend was a purpose that was fulfilling, but I still felt like there was more... something else I was supposed to be doing. Perhaps our legacy is as simple as making sure that all who are in our lives leave our presence in a more positive state. That we touch them with love and kindness, sharing our life experiences to help them face their own. But then there is that thought, lurking deep inside that there is something else. That somehow, we'll find that next level of what we are 'meant' to do. What "He" wants us to become. I felt optimistic about therapy work with Chewie, but I had a nagging sense; there was more I was supposed to be doing. Through my prayer, I continued to ask Him, sometimes even beg... how can I be of service to you today, what do you want from me? The word 'write' kept popping into my mind, and I felt a sense of urgency to capture what I'd experienced these past few years. Perhaps writing this book was my reason for living... beyond my daughter... to share my experiences with others and, hopefully, bring hope to someone who may be facing some life challenges of their own. Illness or strife, it doesn't matter, does it?

We all face things in our life that at the moment seem impossible; for me, it was the ever-presence of pain; for others, it may be a horrible diagnosis, separation or divorce, loss of love, betrayal. The list goes on. Perhaps these experiences shared on paper will give someone else hope. That whatever you are facing, it's going to be okay, that new 'reason' will come to you if you take a little time for silence every day. Stare out at the landscape, find a quiet place in music or nature and ask for help, either out loud to people in your life or in private to Him.

One thing I learned that was more important than anything, was to lean on others even when that leaning, is on a dog.

Signs from Above

I pray all the time... and I have come to let go of the fiercely independent woman I had been, and I ask for help when I need it. I'm honest when friends ask how I am and humbled when they offer to help, which I've learned to accept gratefully. If you're going through a hard time, ask yourself – when was the last time you were honest when someone asked how you were? And if you were strong enough to own your truth, that you accepted help when they offered it?

I came to realize that I needed to take breaks, to step away from the hard work of daily life and explore the world with my family. My job afforded me the luxury of travel, and I had accumulated vacation time, so I decided to take Kajal and my mother back to St. John in the U.S. Virgin Islands, a place we'd traveled to before and truly loved the lushness of this paradise. The last time we had been there, unbeknownst to me, I'd been seriously ill and fighting for my life. I'd spent what should have been our idyllic days, battling horrific migraines and throwing up in the luxury hotel room while my mother and Kajal had to explore the resort on their own. I should have known that something was seriously wrong when after the hotel had left us on the beach while we waited for our room to become available, I'd spent my energy telling off the concierge. When our room was finally ready, and a valet was showing us the way, I had to step off the path where I proceeded to projectile vomit on the perfect landscaping in front of mortified and perfectly dressed hotel guests. The hotel had felt so bad that they gave me enough credits to cover the cost of the room and sent baskets full of gourmet crackers and ginger ale while my family wandered in paradise.

I wasn't thrilled to be parted from Chewie for so long, but I knew we all needed this, and I wasn't so sure he'd survive the heat of the islands, so my friend offered to babysit our animals while we hit the vacation trail. I booked us into a small resort that had always been a dream of ours, Caneel Bay, a resort started by the Rockefeller family to preserve the beaches and natural splendor of the island. I'd reserved a small bungalow right on the beach, and we relaxed together, listening to the waves and enjoying the breathtaking island paradise. I swam in the warm water and found myself praying for spiritual guidance.

Green sea turtles came out of the shadows and swam alongside me, gracefully eating the tall swaying seagrass and gazing at me in a manner that seemed to be full of peaceful wisdom. I swam with them until finally, tired and serene, I walked towards the shore. As the surf curled around my legs, I saw something glistening in the sand, and I reached for it curiously. A piece of white coral, in the shape of a cross, lay in the palm of my hand.

That night I dreamed there was a knock at our cottage door. I opened it to find a man holding a young boy's hand. The boy was young, not more than ten. He was frail, almost bone-thin, and had the saddest eyes I'd ever seen. The man held out the boy's hand and said to me; he has no one... only you. I understood immediately and knew what I had to do.... I took his hand, and as he gazed up at me, I knew I was looking into the eyes of my son.

I woke up and immediately started to write it all down; I did not want to forget. Kajal woke up and asked what I was doing, and I told her every detail. I knew it was like the dream I had of her, almost ten years earlier. I trusted that dream and knew I needed to believe this one. I am not sure how, but I knew once again that I'd prayed for a sign, and He gave one to me... as clear as before. I am not sure how, but I knew that one day, we would find this boy. Kajal was excited and hung on to every word. That is all she ever wanted –family, siblings, a future surrounded by love. I did not doubt that adoption was in our future, again.

Joy

We returned to the 'real' world, and my work took hold of me again as I struggled to hold on to my job. I reached out to the Department of Social Services to start the adoption path again, but it seemed like life once more, got in the way. I focused on the more immediate needs of life and of spending quality time with Kajal. We continued to travel to the Smoky Mountains, where Benita and Patti lived and trained Chewie to save lives through water rescue work. The first time Chewie pulled me through the water as his 'victim,' I hung on to his furry hips as he pulled me through the water to shore. Every few strokes of his massive legs, he would lift his head and look over his shoulder to check on me. I could see in his eyes the concern and the desire to help me, and I was in awe of the skills that seemed to live deep within his bones and his inherited genetic memory. The joy we found playing and working with this magical animal was endless.

We started to do therapy work with him. I could only walk short distances as I continued to build my strength, but the hospital we worked with had enormous patience with us. We were able to take breaks as we needed to and only volunteered for short periods, as even Chewie would grow emotionally and physically drained by the intensity of the work that we did. The pleasure on the faces of patients we visited blew me away and brought me back to the moment a little dog gave me peace when my world was crashing in on me. Chewie made people smile just from seeing him from a distance, never mind when his massive tongue traveled from chin to forehead in one super wet swipe. He was 140 lbs. And he was still growing. Cars pulled over when we walked by, and people from all over the world stopped to take pictures with him and hug him. He brought our family joy we could never have imagined, and he spread that love with everyone he met.

Who could have thought a brain tumor would have been the nightmare that brought this precious being into our lives? We visited with firefighters, police, and sheriff departments, and the hospital was going into the intensive care unit was his favorite place to be. He would drag me toward the entrance in excitement then become serious after the electric doors closed behind us. He just knew this is where he was meant to be. Before we met with patients or their families, he'd focus on the doctors and nurses. They loved on him, patted him, and laughed at his sometimes-silly antics. He would fall to the floor and roll over on his back, throw his huge shaggy arm up in the air and wrap it around the nearest nurse. He'd pull her down as if to ask, want to rub my belly? Then kiss him or her, as he pulled them close. These incredibly talented medical staff poured everything into their patients, so Chewie poured himself into them. He was their angel and, without a doubt, the largest and gentlest therapy dog any had ever met.

I wasn't the same person I was before brain surgery. I did not want to be. My view of life was fresh, God-given, and every breath was incredible to me. Yet even with this new mindfulness about the gift of life I had been given, there was still the 'real' world to contend with. I was under immense pressure at work to deliver more and more each day, but keeping it together was becoming almost impossible. Managing through the pain and acting like everything was alright, when it wasn't, was having its impact. I was exhausted all the time, barely holding it together.

I continued to be excluded from conference calls and meetings, but I didn't push it. Perhaps it was for the best; it was all I could do to get through the day without collapsing. I was able to manage my team as I had done in the past, but my enthusiasm for work being the center of my life had changed. As my assistant, Patty protected me fiercely, I took short naps or found myself sitting in my home office in complete darkness, with only the light of the computer reflected on my face as I tried to keep the pain at bay, throughout the day.

I wasn't working the 18-hour days that I had in the past. I just wasn't capable of it, and I'd finally had to admit to my boss that I needed special accommodations to deal with my constant head pain. I worked in a corporate environment that demanded perfection, and let's not kid ourselves; I was far from it. The reality was that the job was not everything to me. Next to my daughter, all I had cared about 'before' was my career. Now it was more of a means to an end, the position that brought us the financial security we needed to live our lives. I delivered solutions for my clients and exceeded the goals my boss imposed on me, but I could see I was not being treated the same as my colleagues.

My boss kept complaining that I was not working at 100%, that I wasn't the same, but instead of celebrating that I was alive and yes, perhaps changed, they kept pushing for more. No matter what I accomplished, it was never enough. I knew they had already given up on me, and it was just a matter of time until I was forced to leave. I had survived lifesaving brain surgery; how many people can say that? I had returned to work two months later; the only significant change (other than needing to lean on my assistant more for appointment reminders) was that it was not all I wanted to do anymore. I cared more about changing the world than increasing profits, and I spent more time building out programs to help veterans and diverse populations. I did not want the job to be everything anymore unless, within it, I could find ways to help people.

I'd had my wakeup call, and I wanted to embrace life more healthily and spiritually. Be more connected with my daughter, with my family and friends. The desire to travel the world first-class slipped into a craving to learn how to camp in nature. I honestly found more joy in simpler living. I was happy with who I was in the day, not who I had thought I'd wanted, or even needed to be to meet the expectations of the world around me. I lost my job within two years of my surgery. It was what it was, and even though it was handled cruelly (a story for another day), it was a gift, as I would never have had the courage to walk away on my own.

It is almost comical that the same week I was fired, I'd spoken at a conference for business leaders about diversity (including the disabled) and how to attract and retain diverse talent. I had had a standing ovation, and one business executive had even approached me afterward to tell me I had accomplished everything she hoped to in her professional career. If she only knew I was fighting for my job while I had appeared so put together. Working with such increased pressure and stress had just made me sicker. My pain increased in my head until there was rarely a break from it. It felt like the work I was doing was killing me. My company had set me up to fail by treating me differently than my colleagues when I had returned. Our business had been a service business, and executives were responsible for managing and growing their client base.

Within a month of returning from surgery, I was told that it was great to have me back, but I was treated differently than my colleagues, there was no denying it. They were handed new business opportunities while I was expected to obtain my own. I had to work harder to prove myself, and I was left out of strategic planning meetings. My boss communicated directly with the woman who had falsely discredited me during my sick leave, making it almost impossible to manage her or the clients she managed that ultimately, I was responsible for. The writing was on the wall, and I should have known that no matter what I did, it would never have been enough. I was proud of what I'd accomplished with the company, but the inevitable happened, and they found a reason to terminate me. After 15 years of loyalty, I was terminated.

It's okay, I'm getting by, and if anything, it forced me to take the time to rest and heal that I'd never have allowed myself. I have battled depression and anxiety over all the changes in my life and the pain, well, I'm still figuring out how to manage that through medication, meditation, and therapy. I go for weekly neuro head massages to help with pain management, and I have learned to laugh at myself all the time. Words do not always align with what my brain is thinking, and my daughter is often correcting what pops out. Horse instead of house, chair instead of car, toothpaste instead of flowers. It was a guessing game, but we managed to find humor in the errors. I was exhausted from dealing with the pain, but I found joy in every day. I would sit in my garden and watch as Chewie chased bees and butterflies.

I met with a neuropsychiatrist who ran a battery of tests, and the results threw me for a loop. They confirmed the tumor had left me with frontal lobe damage, which made learning new things more challenging. Processing even the most uncomplicated information seemed to be more and more difficult. Focusing for any period was painful, whether trying to pay my bills, follow a conversation, or read a book. The doctor confirmed that I'd established my new 'normal,' I was physically changed forever, and he wanted me to have realistic expectations about my future.

That did not sit so well with me. I may be changed, but I had new dreams, and I was committed to having more children through fostering or adopting, and I knew I had survived for a reason. That purpose was still driving me, spreading love through the work Chewie and I would do together and whatever else God had planned for me. Managing through the pain had been a delicate balancing act through my previous workdays, but now, I had to come to terms with who I was post tumor, not an executive traveling the globe with a brain that worked at lightning speed. I had to redefine myself and learn to be okay with whatever that definition might be. I had always considered myself a highly intelligent woman, and I'd been proud of that intellect and my ability to assimilate information quickly. Who would I be now and going forward in life? How do I redefine the person that I am when such core aspects of 'me' had changed so dramatically? Why do we even need to define ourselves? Why were that business card and title so important, and why, even with a newfound purpose, did I still cling to the old image of who I was and who I had thought I'd been?

I found myself swinging back and forth from excitement for the future and the service work that awaited me to sinking into a dark hole of depression and hopelessness – unsure of where I belonged in the world and wondering who I would be.

Gratitude

When I had the clear-headedness to reach out to my close friend Bill who'd had the foresight to help me get sober so long ago, I'd share about the depression and vent all the ways I was beginning to feel sorry for myself. He'd snap me out of it as the sobriety program had taught us to do by reminding me to write a gratitude list. I hated when that advice was given, as there was nothing more an alcoholic liked to do more than spend time dwelling in self-pity. But instead of swearing at him as I wanted to do and wallowing in all the ways my life had changed and wasn't as beautiful as I'd now convinced myself it had been, I got out the pencil. As the list grew longer and my darkness slipped away, I knew it was time to share some of my newfound gratitude with others who deserved it.

I needed to start with the nurse who had saved my life. I went to the walk-in clinic and asked for the nurse practitioner, hoping she'd remember who I was. I didn't remember her name, but the receptionist was quick to know who I'd described and when she came out to the desk, I thanked her for having the insight to send me for the CT scan that found my tumor. She cried with me and admitted she'd never had to give such bad news. She'd wondered what happened to me, not sure I'd survived. She acknowledged that typically she wouldn't order an emergency CT scan like that, but something nudged her to write the order. She was a woman of faith, and as she gazed at me with tear-filled eyes, she shared that she thought God had pushed her to order the test for me. It just wasn't something she would have done on her own. After she'd seen the results of the CT scan, she had done a massive amount of online homework to learn about meningiomas, so she'd be able to answer any questions I'd had. That's why I'd had to wait so long in the reception area of the diagnostic facility. As prepared as she was for me to ask almost anything, she'd been surprised as I'd asked virtually nothing. I shared that I had been in shock and didn't even know what questions to ask.

After visiting with her, I realized I should also meet the radiologist who took the scan itself, so I drove to that office and asked to see her. The woman came out, barely 25 years old, and I reminded her who I was, and thanked her for being part of the small group of medical professionals who had saved my life. She remembered that day and admitted it was the worst thing she had seen. She didn't know how to react, but after that day, all she could think about was that I'd shared with her I was a single mother and just wanted to get home to my daughter. She did not know if I'd made it and was grateful that I'd shared my miraculous recovery with her. I found myself wondering, how many people are we impacted by every day, whom we don't think to follow-up up with?

This felt like closure for me, another step towards healing... I would be forever grateful for those two people who took the time to care for a stranger, to be part of bringing this single mother home.

One day my therapist (I am all for therapists, don't be shy if you feel you need help. A good therapist can help you by being objective and caring about what is best for you without personal motivations) and I were talking. I'd shared how I was struggling with finding meaning in my life. Nothing I did seemed to make a difference, and I could not make sense of why I was still here. I was doing the work with Chewie and struggling to write my story, but it was a long, painfully slow process.

126

I had not had the energy to pursue the adoption process yet, and my larger purpose seemed unclear and out of reach. I kept hearing of people dying of brain tumors. Why not me? Why was I alive? Why not someone else?

He looked at me and simply said, "Borrowing hope. I use your story to inspire other patients. I don't share your name, but I tell them a little bit of your story, and it gives them hope." I was filled with peace and, finally, a little acceptance of myself, of my worthiness. Maybe, that's what this was all about. My writing this book came from asking the question, what can I do to make a difference? To make sense of all I've lived through. If I can create hope where there is darkness, laughter where there is quiet, then perhaps this was all worth something more than just an extended period of suffering. Wouldn't you think?

Teenage Wisdom

I was shattered from losing my job. My identity aligned with being a successful executive, I couldn't imagine what my life would be without being in that role. I hated getting my hands dirty and enjoyed being a global executive. The 'new' me took time to plant vegetables with my daughter. I learned to cook a burger over an open fire (so maybe it came out raw, and we ate burnt marshmallows instead) and spent hours with my daughter driving through backcountry roads.

I reflected on all the times that business had taken me away from home, and I had missed crucial moments when my family had needed me. There was the time I was in Denmark, and my daughter called me in the middle of the night crying because of a toothache. I had to call on a friend to bring her to the dentist's. She needed me desperately, and I wasn't there, holding her when she needed me. I'd been in China when my brothers and sisters gathered around my father for what we later realized where his final lucid days. So many moments were missed, as I had fought to keep my career together – working for people who did not care for me and for whom the bottom line always took precedence over everything else. What had I been thinking? My priorities had been messed up.

The day I lost my job, and I was reeling from the shock of the way I'd been treated by my company, I realized we had tickets to a concert. I was experiencing significant financial insecurity of an unknown future, and the last thing I wanted to do was go out on the town. I had ordered tickets to our favorite artists, The Piano Guys, and the concert was that evening. It seemed important to put my shock and fear aside and just have a 'normal' night with my daughter. I was walking in a daze but tried to be brave for Kajal's sake. I told her about work and reassured her that everything would be okay, even though my inner thoughts were riddled with fear and self-doubt. The doubt was deeply connected to my physical challenges, to my need for extra rest during the day, and my growing short-term memory issues. If it had not been for my friend/assistant extraordinaire, Patty, who had been my right hand, I'd never have been able to pull off everything I had. She always had my back and had helped keep me organized and on task. Without her, I felt utterly incapable. Who would hire someone like me? My pain had become almost unmanageable; how could I even think about working when I had migraines daily. I had barely kept it together as it was.

I hid my fears and focused on Kajal, and we headed to the concert. The concert was terrific, and we lost ourselves in the incredible, mind-bending cello and piano music. As the show neared the end, our favorite artist, the extraordinary cello player Steven Sharp Nelson stepped up to the microphone. "We normally end our concert with another piece you are all likely expecting, but tonight we've come together as a group and decided to do something different."

"I'd like to share something personal that I haven't shared in a concert before. My mother died of a brain tumor." My heart jumped in my chest, and I immediately choked up in intense emotion. "My father stood by and helped her for years as she fought against it. My father was my hero for all he did to help her survive as she battled the tumor, and he became an incredible single parent after she passed. We received a letter from a young boy," Kajal started tapping my shoulder, but I was leaning forward in my seat locked on to every word ... "who shared with us that his mother had to battle a life-threatening brain tumor and that he truly felt our music had helped her heal." Kajal finally got my attention by grabbing my hand, "Mom, that was me! They don't understand my name is a girl's name!"

130

Tears were now streaming down my face as Kajal took out her phone and showed me the letter she had sent to their management team that she'd tracked down on the internet. Steven continued, "so in dedication to this boy's hero, his Mother; we dedicate this special song." The first notes to Rachel Platen's 'Fight Song' broke out, and I was sobbing now. I was brought back to that MRI in the hospital when I thought I was dying, and this song played in my head. 'How?! Why?!' I asked Kajal through the tears; people around us were staring at us. Kajal confidently answered, "because I wanted them to know how special you are, and how their music played a part in your getting better."

Knowing my daughter was proud of me meant more than my job, more than any paycheck. This was what it was all about. At that moment, I came to believe my own words to her that everything was going to be okay. Our faith was strong, and as we'd already learned, we were not going it alone. We met the artists backstage, and they were incredible, kind, and compassionate. They were blown away that Kajal had reached out to them, and it had touched them deeply. That's why they made their music. They were a faith-based band who had no qualms sharing their faith through their music. It was a gift that they were grateful for and felt a calling to share with the world. Kajal and I left that stadium worry-free, excited for the unknown life that awaited us.

When Kajal first came home from India, she was shattered by the brutality of her life. She was tiny, as she'd stopped growing around the age of 3 due to malnutrition. She had faced the world alone without the love or kindness every child deserves. I remember thinking that the most important gift I could give her was a sense of self-worth. Love didn't seem to be enough; all the hugs and words didn't seem to convey that she was as cherished as she was, and I was too impatient to wait the years that my showing up for her every day would help solidify. A neighbor was in the Air Force and told me about a program where pilots would work with children to teach them how to fly, and I found myself thinking if she could fly, do the impossible, then maybe she would start to believe in herself.

I lined up flight lessons, and sure enough, she was flying her first plane by the age of 8. I asked her one day as we were driving home (after she had landed her first single-engine plane) if she remembered why I'd given her the lessons. "So that one day, if I doubt myself, I can say, I flew a plane when I was eight years old so that I can do anything," she replied. Now, my precious one was taking that lesson and giving it back to me... she was helping me to find value in myself once again – knowing that if all I was in my life, was her mother... then that's all I ever needed to be.

Finding Grace

I've gotten through the worst of it now, the ghosts (or angels as I'd prefer to think of them) have slipped into the darkness. They never told me what they wanted, and I didn't become the next big tv 'thing' talking with dead relatives. Maybe it was just a trick of my healing brain. The monster meningioma that lived in my head silently for so long is gone. I'm starting to live my life again. I'm stronger, happier. I rarely get stressed out (stress is literally painful, so when it starts to creep in and the pressure in my head increases, I lie in darkness until it passes), and when something bad happens, I find myself thinking that I can get through this, it's not a brain tumor. I make ends meet, but I believe that it's going to be okay. I traded in my Lexus for a minivan. I don't worry about leaving the house with or without makeup on, and sometimes, more than others, my hair is a mess.

We got a little sister for Chewie; her name was Amazing Grace, and we were looking forward to training her in therapy and water rescue work too. I was so excited for Kajal. Chewie had truly become my dog, as he had

133

become so protective of me, but we realized there was a reason most Newfie owners had at least two. They needed a playmate their size; life had shown us that rather quickly. Amber had broken her ankle when she jumped off my bed trying to get away from a playful Chewie, and my mother's tiny Papillion Zoey, practically had a heart attack every time Chewie looked her way. He was still more than a little naughty when he got bored, and one day (since we knew enough to keep food off the counters) he had grabbed a small glass bowl and clenching it in his teeth danced around my mother shaking his head, as if to say, come and get it. She'd tried to grab it from him but tripped and fell. The glass bowl had remained unbroken but not my mother's wrist, which she'd thrown out to protect her in the fall.

Even though Kajal was trained as a therapy handler for Chewie along with her water rescue work, she was interested in showing a dog competitively. As beautiful as Chewie was, he wasn't a show dog, he was a service dog. She was so excited about Grace, who was simply magnificent. She had shiny black fur, intelligent eyes, and a blaze of white lightning on her chest. She was graceful and the perfect image of a more elegant Newfoundland. Kajal was more excited than I'd seen her since before my diagnosis. This new puppy was truly hers, and she started training her with every spare moment she had.

Grace learned to ring 'potty' bells (the bells you hang on a door and train dogs to ring so that they can let you know when they need to go outside and do their business). She learned to ring them the first week we introduced them to her before she even left her birth home. Her intelligence and affectionate nature drew us in, and we were totally in love with her. Then just a few weeks after we brought her home, she developed a tiny cough. Our friend, Benita, suggested we have her heart checked just to make sure it wasn't anything serious. We contacted our vet and made an appointment with a specialist to check her out and run some tests. On the day of the scheduled appointment, a snowstorm hit, and everything was shutting down. People were freaking out, literally! The stores were emptying of all the necessary supplies, and businesses were closing for the foreseeable future.

I had never driven in the snow before, so I was a bit nervous but desperately wanted the reassurance that Grace would be alright. I braved the oncoming storm and drove to the vet's office. When I arrived, the receptionist told me that they'd been trying to reach me as the veterinarian couldn't make it and was trapped on the island that was his home, off the coast of Charleston. Are you kidding me?

I packed my little beauty back into the car and made my way very carefully home, praying as I took note of the emptying highways and roads as the snow grew harder and harder. Charleston doesn't have snowplows on hand, so the city pretty much shut down in the face of a quarter-inch of snow, never mind what was potentially a foot. This wasn't Boston; even the salt was gone from all the shelves in the grocery stores as it was all people could access to try and protect their walkways. When we arrived home (safely, thank God), Kajal was bubbling over with excitement. Our usually green landscape was quickly becoming a winter wonderland, and the beauty of the serene whiteness was breathtaking.

Kajal bundled up with the warmest clothes she could find and ran outside to join the other children of the neighborhood for snowball fights and snowman building. A fire was burning in the fireplace; the house was cozy and warm. I watched Kajal as she played with Grace and Chewie in the snow. I hadn't seen her so happy in a long, long time. She was running free, waving her arms and laughing joyfully. Chewie and Grace were enjoying the cold weather as they ran to catch the fast-falling, fluffy snowflakes on their long pink tongues. Worries didn't exist as she played like a child with the love of two animals, rolling on the ground in the fresh white powder. Once again, I found myself counting my blessings… so grateful to be alive and experiencing such simple pleasures with my family. It doesn't get better than this; I found myself thinking, over and over again.

Kajal was an early riser as most of the medicine I take to manage my head pain is in the evening, so it takes me a bit to come out of my morning fog. Her daily chores included letting the dogs into the backyard to do their morning business and putting out their breakfast. Most mornings, she wakes me with a hot cup of coffee to help me start the day. How awesome is she? But this morning wasn't like any other; she called to me to say she was worried about Grace, she seemed to be having trouble breathing and asked if we could take her to the vet later that morning. Of course, I said, but before I could awaken to check what was happening, she told me Grace was doing better and had run outside and was licking at the cold air and having fun with Chewie.

135

Only a short time passed when I heard Kajal screaming. "Mommm! Grace isn't breathing!" She had silently slipped away to sleep in a far corner of our back yard where Kajal had found her. Kajal scooped her little body up and was screaming at the top of her lungs as she ran towards the house. Grace was lying in her arms, her precious baby face so still and her legs unmoving.

"I don't know what to do, MOM!" Tears were streaming down her face, and I pulled Grace from her arms. This can't be real; this can't be happening. I called to her, GRACE! Come on, my baby, wake up! I rubbed her chest and leaned close, praying to feel her warm breath.

She was lying there, limp in my arms, when I noticed a tiny bit of foam in the corner of her mouth. We raced to get dressed, one of us holding Grace always, still rubbing her chest and begging her to live and ran for the car. I drove through the slippery, empty streets as fast as I could, desperate to get her to the emergency vet. The world around us was still, quiet and devoid of life, and all we could think was please God, don't take this precious little soul from us. Tears streamed down Kajal's face as she held Grace, patting her beautiful face… whispering to her, live.

We arrived at the vet, and the technicians were waiting for us. They quietly took Grace from our arms and raced her out of sight. I knew when they came back just a short time later, that she'd passed. Our baby, Grace, was gone. This little perfect and joyful puppy was gone.

We grieved, and my heart broke for Kajal, who had spent the last two years caring for me, studying her heart out, and being responsible beyond her years. Although I knew we could never replace our little Grace, I came to realize that the only way to fill the absence her precious spirit had left behind was to bring home another puppy. We needed the joy they bring with them to quiet the bells we could still imagine ringing and warm the cold sadness that lived in our hearts.

Enter, Abraham, 60 pounds, and just barely 17 weeks. He was not the brightest pup or the most motivated. He was the last one to notice Patti (from TimberKnoll, of course) calling for dinner and the slowest puppy in his pack to play with toys. He seemed like an old soul who just gained pleasure through simple existence, but his perfectly round head and mellow eyes grabbed hold of my daughter's heart, and she was determined to bring him home. He's already drooling like a big boy, and we started his training in hopes that therapy work also lives in his future. We got him his first baby bib (dog bibs are a staple for this gentle giant breed), and Chewie has built up a whole collection, my favorite one reads, "Drool is just a kiss that lingers." If that's not an analogy on life, I don't know what is. All the hell we go through walking in this life is just joy waiting to happen.

Grace's bells still hang on our back door and darned if I don't hear them ring at times when no one else is nearby.

Letting Go, Letting God

It is easy to get caught up in past regrets or worries about the future. Financial concerns or fear of ending up alone can wreck my peace in a heartbeat. I practice staying in the moment through mindfulness and prayer to relieve the stress and find continued joy in simple things. I surround myself with family and friends who believe in me and am grateful for all the love God has brought into my life. I have finally, truly let go of my perceptions of who I thought I was meant to be.

Recovery comes in waves of darkness and light. Anything you are fighting to overcome, loss of a loved one, a job, a dream, illness, or addiction, just know that the pain doesn't last. Joy and love follow if you're willing to hang in there, and as they say in the program that helps keep me sober, don't give up until the miracle happens. Life always throws curves at you, highs and lows. It's not easy for long before another challenge surfaces. But if there was no pain, would we appreciate the simple joys? Would we find our unique spiritual path and feel a genuine connection to God if we weren't brought to our knees on occasion? Isn't it when we are on our knees, desperate and alone that we feel the closest to Him?

They tell you in the meetings I go to, to let go and let God. I hated that for a long time. Trusting a higher power doesn't come easily, especially when you're in a place of hurt or pain. Every day we try to control everything that happens to us. With a million little to-do lists and all the must-haves and must 'be's, the expectations we put on ourselves. It always seems more natural to cling to perceived notions of what you're supposed to be doing and who you're supposed to be doing it with. There are so many pressures we put on ourselves, so many expectations. Imagine letting go of those, finally being free of all that stress.

When you do it, just turn it over to God, then that freedom lifts you up in ways you can't begin to imagine. How do you let go of everything you believed you were supposed to be? I can only share how I did it, by having the willingness to change and to trust, that He may have a better plan for me than I had for myself. What I was hanging on to was not helping me, so why not try something new? I tried to remember to pray every morning, to ask for guidance, and be of service; however, He might need me to be, and things would pop up during the day that would guide me to what I was supposed to do next.

Chewie and I volunteer when we can for the medical network, which owned the hospital where I spent that first 24 hours post-diagnosis. ...where I met little Raider, who gave me hope and comfort in my darkest moments. I'd come full circle, and now Chewie and I would be the ones traveling the hospital hallways in search of patients and medical staff, who need just a little bit of light in their own nightmares.

These past few years of pain and confusion have brought clarity into my soul. When I think about the future, I've started to formulate a new dream that God had planted on my heart. My path, my purpose, was becoming apparent. During my visits with Benita and Patti at their mountain home in Tennessee, surrounded by a dozen bear dogs, we found through conversation and prayer that our paths were meant to cross. Our desire for purpose was not mutually exclusive.

Purpose Found

Through all the years of volunteering for different non-profit organizations and managing a large corporation, I had learned so much. Even with my physical challenges, I could not imagine that knowledge would not have some value. As I reflected on my life, I realized the signs were always there for me, dreams of fostering and adopting more children, the desire to have a therapy dog, even the desire to rescue animals and help veterans. There was a way to bring it all together, but I knew I could not do it alone. If there is just one valuable lesson, I'd learned from having a brain tumor, it was that leaning on others was not only okay but that it made life so much fuller. We were meant to live in a community, helping one another and surviving not alone but thriving with each other.

Kajal and I visited with TimberKnoll in Tennessee as often as possible, and our relationship with Patti and Benita, and our extended Newfoundland family was growing. One day while Patti and I sat on their back porch, watching Chewie and Abraham playing with their Newfoundland family, Patti asked me what I wanted to do with my life now that I wasn't working in corporate America. She knew a bit of what I'd survived and what my physical limitations were. I shared with her my dream of living somewhere that I could bring pet therapy together with children who had experienced illness or trauma. Patti told me about her background in school administration, working with at-risk youth. She'd been at the forefront of animal-assisted therapy herself, having established the first of its kind, in-school therapy program to help teenagers who the system had given up on. She'd managed an extensive school-based dog therapy program that helped at-risk teenagers. The program, Hudson Ambassadors, had resulted from Patti bringing several of their Newfies into the school system where the dogs had provided companionship and motivation for students. The program had helped teach the students to become more responsible in their education, and the reward became the time they spent with these incredible dogs. Through bonding with the Newfs, they began to gain confidence in themselves, and before you knew it, they were all graduating from high school.

Patti's partner, Benita, brought a whole other set of amazing experiences. She's a U.S. Olympic archer and world team member who brought that level of athletic excellence to her more than 20 years of dog training in water rescue and obedience. She was creative and passionate and knew more about Newfoundland dogs and how to care for them than most veterinarians. Thank goodness, she had returned my desperate plea for a Newfie when I was still recuperating from surgery. Somehow her heart knew she could trust this awkward stranger, and now together, we realized a mutual vision and dream, a new purpose.

Sitting on the porch that day, we knew something special was happening and that God had brought us together for a reason much more significant than any of us could have realized at the time. We each had unique skills that complemented the other, and our dreams of helping people through pet therapy could become a reality. What we couldn't do on our own, we could do together.

We found our new mission together through a mutual desire to help people who suffered from trauma and illness, and we became committed to helping through Newfoundland dog pet therapy. If one tiny dog-like Raider could change my life for the better, give me peace in a moment of shattered fear, just imagine what a large group of massive Newfoundland dogs could do? We zeroed in on first responders, veterans, and people overcoming serious illness.

Even the Hudson Ambassadors, who Patti had helped almost 20 years ago, have become passionately committed to this new dream. These extraordinary graduates wanted to pass forward the gifts that had been given to them. They worked diligently for almost a year, training in obedience and therapy handling until they had successfully passed formal evaluations and become registered therapy dog handlers themselves.

TimberKnoll's Spirit Cove was born. We already have 35 Newfoundland therapy teams with close to 100 teams in training who are committed to helping people too. It's incredible how fast this dream has become a reality. The Newfoundland dog community is enormous. These magnificent dogs are known for their massive size but even more so for their gentle hearts. When people meet them, they melt and find joy in their affectionate nature.

We've spent a lot of time with veterans, firefighters, medical workers, EMS, and police officers whose lives of service have brought them so much stress. Wrapping their arms around our huge Newfies seems to bring these brave heroes a level of peace and calm that they need to help overcome the trauma they experience in their daily lives. With the recent Covid-19 pandemic, we've seen the demand for animal-assisted therapy services grow faster than we ever could have imagined. But as the panic and anxiety in the world has spread, we've also seen the good. More and more people are searching for ways to make a positive difference, and we've heard from Newfie owners across the country that want to find ways to get involved, to help make a difference too. As they've learned about what we're doing, they've wanted to join in and help in their communities.

We developed a plan to build a ranch where Newfoundlands and horses could provide therapy services in an environment of unconditional love and healing. I've come to believe that this ranch will be the future of home of my future foster or adopted children, who could benefit from the healing experience of working with trained therapy dogs. We will be close to Duke so that we can help bring joy and stress relief to the patients and medical staff who need us. To help those battling brain tumors and cancer... to share our story and, hopefully, through the telling, help others to have hope and heal.

We dreamed of taking pet therapy a step further by helping those who heal to pass the healing forward just as I was doing, just as the Hudson Ambassadors were doing. By working with rescue organizations, we'd help match up Newfies with first responders or veterans who needed their pets. We could train them to become pet therapy volunteers themselves to help remove the isolation and stress they experience from all the trauma they've had to battle so they could focus on bringing pet therapy to other service members. I know that when I bring Chewie to visit with firefighters, the connection they seem to feel with my massive, hairy dog just about brings me to my knees. As I see Chewie work his magic with servicemen and women and in the hospitals, we visit, it's hard to think of my challenges. My problems slip away when I see joy dawn in the eyes of those we serve.

The ranch could have a few Gypsy Vanners draft horses, who have a similar nature to Newfoundland dogs and are ideal for therapy. I can imagine them running in a pasture and children learning to work with the animals as we teach them about water rescue and therapy work. I truly felt that this was the reason I had lived through all that I had. I knew I wasn't physically capable of working full time as I still had to manage through my daily head pain and memory challenges, but with this team of people, we could come together to make this new dream a reality. Volunteers were already coming forward to help in all the areas we knew we needed help.

I knew Kajal would be going out into the world in just a few years, and I couldn't even begin to imagine not having her in my daily life. Being her mother will always be the greatest gift of my life but sharing my life in a way that could continue to be of service was also critical.

I promised Kajal a little sister or brother once, and I meant to keep that promise. I wanted to find the little boy I had dreamed of; I knew he still waited for me. Just as she once had. In a part of my soul, I knew this plan for a ranch called Spirit Cove would be the place that would help me find him. I wanted to provide children who needed the gift of hope, an opportunity to develop self-worth, just as Kajal had, through love, acceptance, and service.

I am not the same person I was before the brain tumor. I never will be, but I can embrace who I have become. I still have daily neuropathy and migraines, and although most doctors believe they will last for the rest of my life, I also have learned that miracles happen, and with God, all things are possible. I accept the pain as part of who I am now, the price of my survival, so I try to celebrate it versus resent or fear it. I believe that if even

144

a tiny part of my story can help someone else learn to accept and love themselves, love their life even a little bit more, then my anguish and fear, pain and self-doubt was worth it.

I don't want to be defined by a mass of cells that had grown in my head. Would you want to be defined by your hardships, your diseases, or your heartbreaks? No, of course not. We want to be celebrated for our ability to laugh in the face of challenge, love in the aftermath of heartbreak.

More often than not, we allow ourselves to be defined by those who don't know us or our potential. My siblings used to refer to me as the 'flake' in the family. I don't blame them, in the '80s I had big, blond hair and lived in the fast lane with rich and powerful boyfriends who came in and out of my life as fast as the cars they drove. By the time I had settled down per se, it didn't matter that I'd become a successful global executive or raised an amazing daughter as a single mom. I would always be the 'flakiest' among them. Somewhere along the line, I learned to love them and accept them for who they were, without the need to win their approval. The way they saw me did not cloud my vision of myself. Could you do that? It is easier than you would imagine. It is just a conscious decision. Try it right now … what is the definition that holds you back from being happy and joyful today?

Are you facing a significant life challenge? An illness? Do you doubt your ability to be happy, to be fulfilled? Do you ever doubt your place or purpose in the world? Have you had trouble finding love, or are you merely feeling lost? Remember that miracles do happen if you're open to them. That you're loveable because God loves you, and if you're juggling your bills or a loved one is seriously ill or is not treating you well, remember, it's your choice how you respond and react. Will you let them or the circumstances in your life rob you of your peace? I opened my heart and let the love of those who believe in me, lift me up. My faith had kicked in, and my daughter's humor and tenacity as I remembered all she'd survived on the streets of India, and the hugs and wet kisses of my massive, bear-like dogs kept the laughter in my days.

It becomes easier and easier to focus on the joy in each day, instead of letting my health challenges define who I am. I learned to focus on my mission to share the healing power of Newfies with others who also need lifting up. We all have a passion, a purpose that can stir our souls. If you have not found yours yet, don't give up. Keep searching with an open heart and seeking God's guidance. Before you know it, you will find the clarity and spark to make a difference in the world in your own unique and special way.

When I watch the news and see the world ravaged by tornados, fires, and mudslides… I seek the good. When I hear about the tens of thousands of people dying from the COVID virus or demonstrations that lead to violence as people fight to end racial injustice, I seek the good. The neighbors who are bringing food and blankets, the first responders saving a drowning dog or a child from a burning building. When I see the doctors and nurses putting their own lives on the line to work endless hours saving others and the soldiers returning home from months serving oversees, I see the good. It is always there if you look for it.

I remember one Valentine's day when I was feeling sorry for myself for being alone again. I was in a neighborhood store when I saw those boxes of little hearts with goofy sayings on them. They were on sale, and something made me buy a whole stack of them. I was counting my pennies at that time and was behind in my rent, but something encouraged me to splurge. Although I was not sure what I wasn't going to do with them, I felt driven to find someone more miserable than me and pass them out.

I walked up and down Newbury Street in Boston, a street full of elegant, high-end shops and even busier, wrapped in their own world, shoppers. Clutching my plastic bag, I sought out the lonely. If someone had a frown or looked stressed out, I handed them a box and wished them a happy Valentine's day. I got a lot of dirty looks, mind you, but I kept going. Huddled in one doorway, I found two homeless and slightly tipsy men, drinking from their brown bags. I was terrified to approach them but felt an invisible hand pushing me forward. I handed them a stack of boxes and told them someone loved them. As I turned to leave, I heard one say to the other in his harsh Boston slurred accent, "See, I told yah someone loved yah!".

My mother used to say, you are dying from the moment you are born. We are all dying; we just do not know when the final breath will come. Damn, that is depressing, I used to respond. But here is the thing, you can choose to be dying, waiting around for your time to come, letting the ups and downs of life control you, or you can decide to live and focus on the

146

possibilities. I am choosing to live and no matter your prognosis, or the challenges you're personally facing in life… I hope you do too.

So, now, every day is a celebration. I remember to embrace my pain and my dreams because both remind me that I am here to experience them. I dream of the children that I will foster or adopt one day, the dogs and horses who will call Spirit Cove home. I dream of my daughter's adventures in life and the family, friends, and hurt souls who will find hope and healing on the ranch, that I have no doubt we will build. But I do not live in the dreams; I do not live in yesterday or wait for tomorrow to come. I find something to laugh about, someone to love, someone else to make happy. I do not focus on whether the tumor will grow again or my pain. I do not dwell on what I cannot change or control. I accept who I am, and I focus on the possibilities of what I can do, today, to make tomorrow's dream a reality.

Living in the moment is a practice. It does not come quickly; it comes with a focused desire to be present in each moment. Once when Kajal was playing the piano, I watched her and realized she was more at peace than I had ever seen her. I asked her what it was that she enjoyed playing the piano and what she thought about when she played. Her response, "When I'm playing the piano, it's just me. I'm just a girl at the piano, nothing else." Not a survivor from the streets of India or an honors student, or even a daughter. She was just a girl playing the piano. She was so wise, so young. That is the answer, isn't it? Just be.

The Meaning of It All

O ne day I was having coffee with close friends. They asked me what lessons I'd learned from all I'd overcome. We were celebrating my sobriety anniversary and survival from the brain tumor. I didn't take long to answer.

Let go of resentments and know that others' beliefs are theirs and theirs alone. We cannot control other people or allow them to control us; we need to learn to accept them as we would want to be accepted.

Own and celebrate who we are in this moment, not who we thought we should be, and know without question that all the potential of the world lives within us.

Trust that God has your back ... He is always there, just waiting to be called on to guide you through your day.

Just take the time to find your quiet place, stop, and listen. If you're willing to change and open to asking what your purpose is. The answers will come; they always do.

Know that you are loved and that most of all, you are loveable.

Be willing to ask for help when tough times hit. Realize that you are not alone, you will be amazed by how many people care about you and will show up right when you need them. Accept the help when it is offered, it doesn't mean you are weak; it means you are strong.

Be kind to every person who crosses your path and help others, in whatever way you can. Whether it is bringing supplies to a family who is struggling, delivering a meal to someone going through a difficult time, or driving a neighbor's child to school when they are fighting an illness.

If we embrace this knowledge, spread, and accept love, how can we not find true peace and joy in every day?

My friend smiled and handed me a gift bag, I pulled a delicate bracelet out and read the finely engraved letters… 'Be the light.'

It is not the end...
It's only the beginning.

Pet Therapy Information

To learn more about TimberKnoll's Spirit Cove or pet therapy,
Please visit:

NewfieTherapy.org

You can also email us at Info@NewfieTherapy.org

Special Dedications

Kelly and Raider, who visited Lisa in the hospital emergency room.

Hudson, Ellie, Oscar, and Tess. The original Hudson Ambassador therapy dog team helped inspire TimberKnoll's Spirit Cove.

The Hudson Ambassadors, who are the heart of Spirit Cove, with Lisa,

Patti, and Benita. Celebrating passing therapy dog evaluations with their pet partners, Milan, Greyson, Bentley, Ella, Sunee, Amelia, Rook & Benjamin.

Made in the USA
Columbia, SC
07 February 2025

52575932R10102